Praise for *How to Raise a Citizen*

"In *How to Raise a Citizen,* Cormack explores the urgent need for effective civic attention in our homes. With democratic engagement at a critical juncture, this book serves as a guide for parents striving to fill the gaps left by formal education systems in political and civic understanding. This book provides practical strategies to help parents pass on the foundational knowledge every young adult should have before stepping out into the world in order to be as powerful as possible. More importantly, it emphasizes the skill of engaging in respectful, informed discussions, a key component of democratic participation. *How to Raise a Citizen* is more than just a parenting guide—it's a tool to nurture the next generation of informed, engaged, and responsible citizens, ready to contribute to a more functional democracy."

—Dolly Chugh,
author of *The Person You Mean to Be* and *A More Just Future,*
professor at the NYU Stern School of Business

"We all have the power to build a better democracy—and it begins at home. But if it feels like the only thing more complicated than parenting is our polarized and complex political system, Lindsey Cormack makes the never-more-essential task of civics education come alive in this passionate and nonpartisan how-to manual for inspiring our kids about the possibilities of democracy. Bonus point: It doubles as a master class for parents, as well. Our politics might be brutish, and too many Thanksgiving dinners have been ruined by red vs. blue food fights. But what Cormack understands is that democracy dies in silence, and that parents need to do this job because no one else will. Follow her advice and something important will be fun, get your kids talking, and maybe inspire them for life. Our national conversation starts with you."

—David Daley,
best-selling author of *Unrigged: How Americans Are Battling Back to Save Democracy*

"Cormack makes a compelling case that parents play a vital role in raising engaged citizens. This comprehensive guide is a must-read for parents who know our kids need to be more involved in our democracy, but don't know where to start."

—Julie Lythcott-Haims,
New York Times bestselling author of *How to Raise an Adult*

"This book will inspire parents to raise civically minded children in a me-first world. Written by a sensitive parent and political scientist, it offers practical guidance for discussing politics and government with children in a way that prepares them to become balanced, active citizens instead of passive or polarized ones."

—William J. Doherty, PhD,
professor of family social science at the
University of Minnesota and co-founder of Braver Angels

"I've already started incorporating Lindsey's tactics from *How to Raise a Citizen* in my parenting! My 1-year-old daughter and 5-year-old-son are listening and engaging in conversations about voting, political leadership, and the issues they care most about. I hope many parents take on this incredible responsibility as we shape the next generation of voters, policymakers, and political leaders."

—Sara Guillermo,
CEO of Ignite

"In this timely, readable book, Professor Lindsey Cormack reminds us that preserving democracy requires purposeful, lifelong learning and practice. Yet, we often fail to equip our children with the knowledge and tools they need to become empowered citizens. With practical wisdom and relatable advice, Cormack provides parents with a roadmap to help their children grow into adults capable of fixing our broken politics and safeguarding our democratic traditions."

—Andrew Buher,
Princeton University

"Breaking away from traditional parenting or how to understand politics books, Lindsey Cormack takes the reader on a journey that provides parents conversational structures and topics to use with their children when talking about politics. The age-appropriate guides and multiple topic areas Cormack discusses for federal, state, and local-level politics serve as a nice introduction for understanding how politics works and how we can get engaged in politics with our children."

—**Dr. April Chatham-Carpenter**,
professor and department chair, Department of
Applied Communication, University of Arkansas,
Little Rock; Braver Angels national volunteer leader

"A parenting book like no other, *How to Raise a Citizen* offers a nonpartisan toolkit for parents trying to raise kids who become not just good adults, but effective, civically engaged citizens."

—**Elizabeth Doll**,
director of Braver Politics at Braver Angels

"In this timely and much-needed book, Lindsey Cormack, an expert on American politics, reminds us that the responsibility of parenting our democracy didn't end with the founders of our country: it's all our responsibility to pass the torch of democracy on to the next generation by parenting our children to be effective democratic citizens. Readers of Cormack's imaginative book will learn why it's important for parents to accept this core responsibility, how they can raise children to be more effective citizens, and how they can keep democracy's light burning bright by doing so."

—**David Darmofal**,
University of South Carolina

"This book is an absolute revolution! *How to Raise a Citizen* is an incisive and easy to follow roadmap for a saner political future for us and our kids."

—**Brandon Rottinghaus**,
professor of political science, University of Houston

"With the heart of a parent and the rigor of a social scientist, Lindsey Cormack guides us through how to prepare our children for the rewards and challenges of citizenship in the twenty-first century. If we follow her advice, we will create a better democracy, one child at a time."

—**Christopher A. Cooper**,
Madison Distinguished Professor of Political Science and Public Affairs, Western Carolina University

"Lindsey Cormack has written the guidebook parents need to help their kids cut through the political noise and to understand our complicated governance system. That's an achievement and a great service."

—**Kevin R. Kosar**,
editor, UnderstandingCongress.org.

"Lindsey Cormack has shown an in-depth understanding of our national and state governments and our political system since high school. It has been her lifelong passion as a student, a professor, and now as a parent. In *How to Raise a Citizen*, Professor Cormack gives parents, and dare I say teachers new to the profession, the who, why, what, and how to overcome the continued decline in knowledge of our government and political system. Rather than 'fearing and avoiding,' Cormack strives to help us 'understand and embrace' politics. Lindsey Cormack's book, *How to Raise a Citizen*, helps us keep our republic."

—**Ken S. Thomas**,
executive director, Johnson County First Amendment Foundation, Kansas First Amendment Foundation

"This book offers a blueprint for parents, blending meticulous research with practical advice, to ensure that family discussions about politics nurture informed, engaged future citizens capable of safeguarding and enriching democracy in America."

—**Yphtach Lelkes**,
associate professor, Annenberg School for Communication and Political Science, University of Pennsylvania

"Professor Lindsey Cormack reminds us that saving our democracy starts at home. *How to Raise a Citizen* is a vital resource for parents who want their kids to be curious, informed, and engaged."

—Christian Vanderbrouk,
contributor to *The Bulwark* and former George W. Bush appointee

How to Raise
a Citizen
(And Why It's Up
to You to Do It)

How to Raise a Citizen (And Why It's Up to You to Do It)

Lindsey Cormack

JB JOSSEY-BASS™
A Wiley Brand

*To my child, and to yours—may they grow to lead
with knowledge and know-how.*

Contents

Acknowledgments

This project has been one of the best experiences of my life, and it would not have been possible without the support and insight of many incredible individuals. I firmly believe that educating our children about the government that governs them is necessary for creating a fair and just society. Everyone deserves to know the rules of the game that they are playing. And although reaching this reality is challenging in our current context, I am inspired by the dedication of parents everywhere who strive to better the world for their children and work to prepare their kids to be as powerful as possible.

I extend my biggest thanks to my daughter, who has patiently listened to various iterations of this project over the years. My gratitude also goes to my undergraduate students, both those well versed and those less familiar with the subject, whose perspectives have underscored the importance of this work. I owe a special thank you to the Stevens Institute of Technology for providing both the environment to explore this field and the sabbatical that was instrumental in completing this project.

My research assistants—Alana Schmitt, Madison Russo, Jenna Booth, Stephanie Ross, Elizabeth Garcia, and Matthew Roberts—were invaluable in conducting numerous interviews and aiding in various aspects of the research for this manuscript.

I am also grateful to have some of the best colleagues—Kristyn Karl, Ashley Lytle, Nancy Nowacek, and Lainie Fefferman—who stepped in to take over things in my absence and who have supported the development of this book and our greater efforts in creating a robust college experience for our students.

I owe an enormous debt of gratitude to my high school social studies and government teacher, Ken Thomas, for setting me on this path. Likewise, I am grateful to my University of Kansas professors—Erik Herron, Fiona Yap, Scott Harris, and Dorothy Pennington—for expanding my knowledge beyond what I learned in high school and for making my dream about a role in academia achievable. I also extend my thanks to the faculty of the NYU politics department, specifically Jonathan Nagler, Patrick Egan, Sandy Gordon, and Howard Rosenthal, for their belief in me throughout the PhD program.

My editor, Kelly Clancy, was the best person I could have worked with for understanding and refining the writing of this book; and my agent, Amanda Bernardi, has significantly enhanced the entire book process. The text has been made cleaner and clearer by Julie Kerr. Everyone I've worked with at Wiley, Jossey-Bass, and High Line Literary Collective has been good to me and I'm thrilled they have believed in this project.

I would also like to thank my friends and family, who have heard me talk about this project for years. Elizabeth Shah and Niral Shah heard many different ideas and helped refine my thinking; they have also cared for me and my daughter in a way that let me have more time to write. Melodia Gurevich has been the biggest cheerleader and amplifier of this project. Kevin Hylant and Madison Telles have been the biggest personal supporters for me during this process. Nicole Ryan and Sarah Vacchiano have inspired me to just do the work I wanted to do.

To those who have shown me the power *and* limits of local government and organizing—especially Tricia Shimamura, Dov Gibor, and Patrick Bobilin—thank you.

My book and dinner club members Michelle Durham, Patricia Durham, Rachel Spooner, Meagan Dobler, Ilana Goldfarb, and Rebecca Mulder have been willing political conversationalists during this effort. Matt Cormack has been a co-parent and person open to modeling how to talk about politics in front of and with our daughter. And I should thank all the other people—both in person and online—who have let me tell them the three-minute version of this book, I have learned so much from getting feedback from others.

I am thankful that the final stages of editing were made so much sweeter with flower deliveries. Having my days brightened with blooms continued to remind me of the process of growth and care.

In a world where many feel that aspects of our politics are broken, I maintain hope in the democratic system and the ongoing experiment that is the United States. Parents have the best opportunity to act as agents of change. By stepping in and stepping up, they can help mend our politics by taking on the challenge of talking about these things with their children.

How to Raise
a Citizen
(And Why It's Up
to You to Do It)

Introduction

I started writing this book when my daughter, nicknamed Bunny, was eight years old. Throughout her life, I've read numerous "how-to" books: how to establish a sleep routine, how to do potty training, how to handle tantrums, how to teach her to read, and how to brace for the challenges of adolescence. However, along the journey of raising her, I realized there was a significant gap in both our how-to books and society. We do not have collective habits in how to prepare children to be engaged, active participants in our democracy.

Every year, I get to engage with a new set of 18- to 22-year-old students in my Introduction to U.S. Politics class. My younger students have just ventured out of their family homes and are learning to run their own schedules, take care of themselves, and navigate the world with increased independence. My older students are more focused on securing their future after college, having already become adept at managing these daily tasks. Regardless of age, up until this point, most of my students haven't had intentional discussions with any adults, including their parents, about what it means to be a citizen.

Many of our college-aged students don't know how to vote, haven't read the Constitution, aren't aware of the local political offices responsible for quality-of-life decisions, lack understanding of the division of responsibilities, have never pondered the concept of federalism, and have formed their view of the court system based on television dramas. It's not anyone's fault in particular, but collectively, we all bear some responsibility.

I don't mean to place blame on parents by pointing this out. In many ways, today's parents have been let down by school systems and social norms that didn't prioritize civic education during our own upbringing. However, parents have an essential role to play in rectifying this situation. Given the broken state of our politics, it's necessary that parents step up to the task.

It wasn't until I began to be asked by elementary schools to prepare civics lessons that I truly considered writing a book for parents. I had the inkling that something like this would be helpful after five or so years of teaching college students who do not know the difference between the House and Senate, but it was in working directly with younger kids that I knew something like this needed to be written.

The purpose of this book is to provide parents with a framework for having discussions about government and politics with their children in a way that feels fun and connective. It's also meant to encourage you to do this work.

As parents with children under 18, we are all raising citizens, but often not *intentionally*. Many of us belong to the Gen X, Millennial, and now Gen Z cohorts, who were discouraged from discussing politics to avoid disagreements and often lack a lot of political and government knowledge ourselves.

In a time when politics feel contentious, if not disastrous, the ability to pass on civic know-how and model how to have difficult conversations are incredibly important things to give to our kids. By being capable and willing to talk about politics and government with our children, we empower them to navigate politics successfully and in turn lead better lives.

As I often tell my students, *politics is going to happen to us whether we like it or not, so we might as well understand how the system works.*

Political discussions make many of us uncomfortable, and some of us were brought up believing that these topics were off-limits. This must change. While many assume schools will adequately teach students how to hold elected officials accountable through voting, or even the very basics of our system, the reality falls short. As parents, we have to step in. If you feel like you don't know enough about government yourself, get ready to put that feeling away, because none of this is that hard to understand. When you're done with this book you will be ready to talk about politics and government with your kids and hopefully be convinced that you'll be doing them an enormous favor in doing so.

Talking About Politics and Government Doesn't Have to Feel Bad

As someone who works in and studies this field professionally, I assure you that politics doesn't have to feel as dire as it sometimes does. As a mom and a professor of politics, I understand what it takes to talk to kids about politics, and in this book, I will guide you on what we, as parents, need to meet this moment. But I also know it's an uphill battle, because for many of us politics and government are things we avoid talking about.

For many of us even the mention of politics is annoying. Sure, sure, *following the news* is important, but understanding or caring about politics? That's pointless! Nothing ever changes! It's picking the least bad of two awful candidates! It's all rigged! They only care about themselves! It's the dirtiest industry there is! Nothing I do matters, why should I care?

These are exactly the thoughts that allow us to have the politics that we do. And many of those who are in positions of power now are just fine with that. The fewer people who know the rules, the less oversight any member of the government has. That's not good, and it's certainly not the world I want to be living in. It's not good for us parents, and it's not good for our children.

Things feel bad when we don't understand them; they feel out of control when we feel insignificant and unable to change things and things are not going "our way." I get why politics can feel like that for many of us. There's also a winning or losing aspect of elections that can be defeating if you find yourself on the losing end.

To start, try thinking about politics as a moving pendulum rather than a set game that is won or lost. Politics is certainly a game, but not one with fixed or forever "winners" and "losers." It's a game that we influence, and we can change. It's a pendulum in that it's forever moving, but unlike a clock that is set to tell time consistently, the forces that move the system are people who move inconsistently. There will be times that feel like wins and times that feel like losses, but knowing that the outcome is not preordained and instead up to us to shape is quite powerful to consider.

Talking politics can feel bad because we might disagree with someone, or not have a common starting point, or feel out of our depth in the discussion because it might be complicated. But here's the thing, no one ever *knows* everything about a political issue—or really any issue. We don't need to go into political discussions thinking we need to "win" or be right. Doing that only increases the likelihood that there are expectations and the potential for huge letdowns anyway. Instead of succumbing to feelings of despair, distrust, and outrage when you hear the word *politics*, try to think about a political discussion as a way to learn something new about a topic or at least the way another person views the topic.

It's truly an amazing power to be alive in a democracy today, but it's one that many of us decide to opt out of because it *feels* bad. But that doesn't have to be the case. If you work to reorient your perspective on politics and government, as something to learn and pass on to your kids, it can actually feel pretty great. You will be doing yourself a service, and one for your kids as well as the wider community. This book aims to guide you through the process with patience and provide you with the tools to navigate politics in a more informed and empowered way.

You might not consider yourself the epitome of an always voting, always engaged citizen, but that shouldn't discourage you from working on your parenting skills in this area. We are all living our own unique forms of citizenship and learning how to exercise our own power. By imparting these lessons to your children, you not only strengthen your own abilities but also theirs.

Partisanship and Polarization

It's hard to escape the sense of fractiousness and polarization in our politics. Most of our media exacerbates this feeling with demonizing headlines, despair, outrage, and personally insulting debates meant to show us who's "right" and "wrong." And partisanship—the labels of Republican and Democrat—dominates national politics.

As you read this book, you'll notice it's not about raising children to align with a particular political party, but about raising engaged and informed citizens. I'm confident that parents with their own political leanings will find opportunities for discussions about partisanship. But I'll note that emerging research suggests that attempts to steer our children toward a specific political party can backfire.[1]

This doesn't mean that partisan divisions and polarization aren't pressing issues—they are. However, one way to address the ugliest aspects of our politics is by better understanding the underlying structures. Regardless of your political orientation, knowing how our government is structured is valuable because it allows you to better understand why things do or do not happen, and what you can do to change that. When children have a more comprehensive view of government and politics, they can develop their own political agency, and that's really what we want for our kids. Raising a child is all about giving them the tools to act as their own agent of their lives; by equipping them to understand politics, we give them another form of power.

My focus is on ensuring that everyone who is entitled to participate in and be affected by the outcomes of our political system understands the rules of the game. And because it's often the young and newly eligible voters who miss out on this knowledge, it's up to us as parents to work on remedying things. Our efforts as parents should focus on establishing a baseline of knowledge and encouraging our children to contemplate fundamental questions about government while teaching them how to have conversations on difficult subjects.

This Might Sound Like a Lot of Work . . .

Before we jump in, let me make one thing clear: I'm not here to add to the overwhelming and never-ending list of parenting expectations. My goal isn't to dictate how or when you should discuss politics with your kids. Instead, I want to encourage you to maintain an ongoing and open dialogue while giving you the strategies and knowledge to do so.

In today's parenting, there's often a tendency to shelter children from difficult situations and shield them from having to think about hard topics. While this approach may enhance their physical safety, it can also hinder their ability to navigate the complexities of life that previous generations of children had to face. Parents unintentionally shield their kids from tough topics by avoiding discussions about current events or controversial political issues altogether.

Let's say there's a significant political event happening in the country, such as a presidential election. Instead of engaging their children in age-appropriate discussions about these topics, many parents might choose to avoid the topic completely, believing that the kids are too young or that it's not their place to be involved. Parents may avoid watching the news or discussing such matters in their household, effectively limiting their children's exposure to different perspectives and critical-thinking opportunities. While the intention might be to protect the child's innocence or maintain a sense of stability, it can result in a lack of understanding and awareness about the world around them, ultimately depriving them of the chance to develop their own informed opinions and participate as a citizen.

Though shielding means that parents may avoid uncomfortable discussions, the strategy just doesn't work in the long run. Kids have a way of finding out about politics, whether it's through overhearing a news broadcast while visiting a grandparent, scrolling through social media, listening in on conversations between older siblings and their friends, or engaging in discussions with other children at school. Children are sponges, absorbing information from their surroundings. So, even if we try to shield them, they will inevitably stumble upon political topics. That's why it's better for us, as trusted sources in their lives, to be the ones who help them approach these topics in a thoughtful and age-appropriate manner.

Just like with discussions about drugs and sex, avoiding politics won't keep our children in the dark. They will find out from other sources, and those sources may not provide accurate or balanced information—just ask a history teacher about how TikTok influencers are changing their jobs in the classroom. As parents, we have the opportunity to create a safe and calm setting where we can discuss politics and government with our children, providing them with a rooted understanding of these topics over a long time horizon. We can establish ground rules, share our knowledge and perspectives, and help them navigate the complexities of the political landscape. While we can't control the eventual outcome or their ultimate opinions, we can give them the tools to make informed decisions and participate in civic life.

Chapter Map

This book is structured for your convenience, allowing you to select sections that align with your specific needs. The first sections describe the current level of political knowledge among our youth and underscore why schools fall short in delivering adequate civic education. I then make the case for why parents should be agents of change, and present frameworks that show parents how to do that.

The second part of the book serves as a politics and government primer, offering a refresher on the basics of our system. If you feel the need to brush up on certain topics before getting into conversations with your children, this section will provide you with the necessary information. Already consider yourself a constitutional buff? Great! Then you've got a good way to start on that topic with your kids and you can instead dive in on other topics that you might not feel so secure in.

Chapter 1 sheds light on the concerning lack of knowledge about politics and government among the general population. Decades of research show a disheartening truth: fewer than half of U.S. adults possess a basic understanding of our government's structure. As federal politics often dominates the headlines, the lack of awareness regarding local and state governance is even more glaring. A significant number of people struggle to name their state representatives, identify their state's governor, or grasp the legislative processes within their own state.

This dearth of political knowledge poses a problem as it directly affects participation, particularly among first-time and younger voters. When people don't fully comprehend how the electoral system operates, they are less likely to engage and exercise their right to vote. And this is detrimental to our democracy.

In this chapter, I discuss various issues associated with an underdeveloped understanding of politics. Limited civic participation is one consequence, as is vulnerability to manipulation and misinformation, as well as the erosion of trust in government. The repercussions of our civic deficit extend beyond mere mistrust and misunderstanding. Unfortunately, we have witnessed incidents in recent years where mistrust of government has escalated into acts of intimidation and violence. If a significant portion of the population feels disengaged and disempowered, our political system will end up representing only the interests of a dedicated few, leaving many others feeling resentful. This not only harms our society but also exacerbates existing inequalities. It's a problem worth paying attention to as a parent.

In Chapter 2, I outline the reasons behind our deficit in political know-how: the complexity of the U.S. system, a generational aversion to discussing politics, ineffective strategies for political conversations, and the misplaced reliance on schools to teach political knowledge.

The first hurdle is the complexity of our political system. It can be overwhelming, especially for people who are not deeply involved in politics, to fully grasp the workings of our system. But fear not! In the second part of this book, I'll show you that there are fundamental pieces of information that can empower even the greenest novices among us to become effective and competent citizens.

Second, there is historical taboo surrounding political conversations. Outdated etiquette rules, many rooted in the nineteenth century, discouraged criticism, nuanced discussions, and the exploration of different opinions. These so-called "politeness" norms have hindered our ability to engage in open discourse. Without this sort of practice in place for generations, a lot of us parents simply don't know where to start. I emphasize the need to challenge these norms and engage in conversations about the governance of our country. I address the common tendency for parents to shy away from discussing politics with their children. While age-appropriate discussions are important, completely avoiding political issues can limit a child's understanding of the world. We need to introduce fundamental concepts of citizenship, democratic values, and respectful engagement, gradually expanding the discussions as our children grow older.

Third, we have an issue with our discourse. Problems arise when we don't talk politics at all with our children *or* when we get wrapped up in the negative, and oftentimes denigrating, side of things. When we focus solely on the negative aspects of politics and government, we inadvertently discourage our children from considering careers in these fields. But as parents, we want to inspire them to become future leaders who can tackle society's greatest challenges. We need to teach them about the process. Instead of exposing them primarily to sensational news headlines based on outrage and knee-jerk reactions, parents can provide a balanced perspective that instills curiosity and a desire to actively participate.

Finally, our schools are not up to this task. Many dedicated educators would love schools to be robust sites of civic learning, but pressures to increase test scores and the fear of blowback from angry parents have forced many schools to scale back their civic focus.

Chapter 3 argues that it's time to recognize the incredible power we have as parents to be catalysts for change. Whether we've hesitated due to concerns about politeness, frustrations with the state of politics, or even our own uncertainties, we need to understand the importance of engaging our children in political conversations. Our goal should not be to raise children who simply echo our political beliefs, but to nurture informed and engaged citizens who can think critically and form their own conclusions.

As parents, we can engage in *years* of meaningful conversations with our children. We must provide our children with the tools and knowledge to talk about politics confidently and navigate our complex systems. Leaving this void unfilled and allowing others to shape their views is not a promising approach. Just like discussing important topics such as drugs and sex, having a trusted guiding hand when it comes to politics is necessary. And that's where parents step in. By initiating conversations about politics and government early on, we can shape the way our children dream, think, and create a brighter political environment for everyone. It may seem daunting at first, but it's a responsibility we should embrace.

In Chapter 4, I provide a set of frameworks to have meaningful conversations about politics and government with your kids. Whether you're a political enthusiast or feel uncertain about these topics, you'll find valuable guidance to navigate these discussions.

If you're passionate and well informed about politics, seize the opportunity to share your expertise and help your kids understand different perspectives. If you have reservations or lack familiarity with political topics, don't let that discourage you. This chapter emphasizes the importance of overcoming hesitations and offers strategies for researching and learning together with your children. Remember, this is a journey of exploration and growth for both you and your kids.

While some topics may be more challenging to discuss with children, this chapter doesn't just provide you with a static script or a checklist of topics to cover. Instead, it's a set of adaptable conversation structures that you can use. These structures will allow you to address a wide range of emerging topics, whether it's issues of political violence and war, expression and equality, or opportunity and prosperity. The goal is to give you a set of starting points that can be customized to fit any conversation.

To ensure that the conversations are age appropriate, I provide guidance on what to discuss with children of different ages. Drawing insights from political socialization research, I categorize discussions into three age groups: young grade school kids (ages 5–9), preadolescents and young adolescents (ages 10–14), and more independent teenagers (ages 15–18). By tailoring the conversations to each age group's specific needs, you can provide information that is suitable for their developmental stage. This chapter also gives examples of how kids can influence politics, even when they're not yet eligible to vote.

In the second part of the book, Chapters 5–9, I'll dig into what your children need to know before they step out into the world to be informed participants in our political system. I'll provide you with a set of basic concepts and details that will empower your kids to handle politics with ease, regardless of where they choose to make their lives. These chapters serve as a guide for anyone looking to refresh their knowledge and understanding of politics and government.

Chapter 5 first spells out the things that you and your kids need to know to be as effective in politics as possible. If you take nothing else from this book, take that list and make sure you and your kids figure out a way to understand the five necessary things to know to make sense of our politics. The chapter then gets into the foundational principles that shape the U.S. government. This includes concepts like republicanism, democracy, and majority rule—the fundamental ideas that help us understand how our government works. This chapter is designed to make things more accessible for parents, making it easier for you to answer your children's questions. By getting a grasp on the basic principles, you'll be quicker to figure out specific political issues because you'll have a working framework for bigger picture questions.

Voting is at the heart of democracy, and Chapter 6 is all about demystifying the process. From understanding how to register and participate in elections to exploring different election structures like primaries and caucuses you'll leave this chapter with the knowledge needed to engage in the electoral process effectively.

In Chapter 7, I explain the components of the U.S. Constitution. I provide an overview of the core document and its amendments, giving you and your kids a solid understanding of this essential document that shapes our government.

Chapter 8 examines federalism and the division of power between the federal, state, and local governments. While national politics often grab the headlines, it's necessary to recognize the significant work happening at the state and local levels. In this chapter, I discuss the roles and responsibilities of each level of government, shedding light on how they work together to serve the needs of the people.

By understanding who is responsible for what, you and your kids can make informed decisions and know whom to reach out to when you want to make a change in your community. You'll also find that if you investigate the local politics in your area, most of the people operating at that level don't seem as monstrous as the stories that we are told about federal politicians. Most of the people serving in government—whether in elected or appointed positions—truly believe that they are trying to make their part of the world better and generally try to do right by those who elected them to power.

Finally, in Chapter 9, I conclude with a hopeful outlook on the transformation that can occur in American politics with more interested and prepared participants. I address the common misconception that politics is pointless and emphasize that it is, in fact, practical for shaping our communities and laws. I highlight the significance of political preparedness in tackling the complex issues our society faces. By becoming knowledgeable and engaged, we can bridge the gap between our wishes and making real change happen.

No matter your political persuasion, knowledge is key to fully realizing your share of political power. And when it comes to specific political goals, involving your whole family in the process makes it even more impactful. Your own kids likely have ideas for improvements they'd like to see in their communities, whether it's more park space, a later school arrival time, or healthier lunch options. By engaging in discussions about politics and government, you can help them bridge the gap between their aspirations and making change happen.

What Is a Citizen? A Note on Terminology

When I use the term *citizen*, I'm referring to it in the most general sense. It's not about legal markers or exclusivity based on age, gender, race, ethnicity, religion, nationality, or sexual identity. These boundaries between citizen and noncitizen are sometimes used to determine who can wield legitimate power in a political system.[2] Instead, I view a citizen as someone with agency within a political system, someone who understands how to activate and use their own power. Citizenship, in this context, goes beyond formal political actions like voting or running for office. It's about being a member of a community, contributing to our shared life, and understanding the governing apparatus in order to engage and support or oppose others within the system.

Children are often seen as "citizens-in-waiting," learning and developing their understanding of politics. In the ways of formal politics—voting, running for office, donating to campaigns—citizen-capable power is only wielded by people old enough to participate.[3] While children may not have the formal rights and responsibilities of adult citizens, they still hold their own forms of political power. Power flows through all of us, regardless of age, as we participate in institutions, organizations, and narratives. That's why it's important to intentionally raise children who understand how to navigate and engage with the system we live in.

Conclusion

This book aims to tackle an often-overlooked aspect of parenting: preparing our children to be engaged and active citizens in our democracy. As parents, we devote our attention to various aspects of our children's growth, but rarely do we find resources that guide us in navigating the complex world of politics with them. That's where this book comes in, offering you the tools, knowledge, and strategies to have meaningful conversations about government and politics with your children.

Unlike the books that exist to help parents raise "successful" or "ivy league-bound" children, this book is different: it is intended for parents who are raising children, period. In 2020, about 65% of high school graduates decided to pursue college, but 100%—whether they liked it or not—have been and will continue to be a part of politics. We're all in this system regardless of educational attainment, job status, or any other markers of adulthood. If we choose not to participate, politics still happens with us and through us—just maybe not in a way that we want. Our bodies count in the Census every 10 years to justify a host of governmental spending and activities. Our dollars count in the form of taxes levied. If we choose to opt out of the system because of ignorance, fear, or apathy, we open possibilities for outcomes that may not go our way.

We all play a role in raising citizens, and it's imperative that we do it with intention and purpose. As parents, we have the power to give our children the skills and understanding they need to be active participants in our democracy.

Engaging our children in discussions about politics goes beyond teaching them about the government and democratic processes. It's about nurturing their critical-thinking skills and their ability to have respectful and constructive conversations, even when the topics are challenging. These skills will shape the future of our society and empower our children to make a positive impact.

In a time when politics may seem polarized and overwhelming, I want to emphasize that there is hope. Together, we can create a future that is more functional and efficient. Politics shouldn't be feared or avoided; instead, it should be understood and embraced. Thank you for taking the time to explore this subject, and I hope you and your family find joy in the process of learning and discussing politics together.

Notes

1. Dinas, E. (2014). Why does the apple fall far from the tree? How early political socialization prompts parent-child dissimilarity. *British Journal of Political Science* 44 (4): 827–852.
2. Nolas, S.-M., Varvantakis, C., and Aruldoss, V. (2017). Talking politics in everyday family lives. *Contemporary Social Science* 12 (1–2): 68–83.
3. Kennelly, J. (2011). Policing young people as citizens-in-waiting: Legitimacy, spatiality and governance. *The British Journal of Criminology* 51 (2): 336–354.

The Civic Know-How Crisis: Causes, Consequences, and the Role of Parents

1

The State of the Citizenry and Risks of Civic Disengagement

Each fall my university works to get students informed about upcoming elections. In my role, as a professor of an Introduction to U.S. Government, I lead a "Students to the Polls," collaborating with school administrators, student organizations, and Greek life to encourage first-time voters to cast their ballots. The exercise is not about which candidates or measures our students support, but simply about establishing the process and habit of voting.

I'm lucky to work at a place with great students. They are young adults who really know how to "do school," they tested well to get in, and many of them eventually go on to remarkable careers. Yet without fail, on Election Day, a good number of them leave crestfallen, having been turned away from the polls for not being registered to vote. I always push students to then cast provisional ballots, but the experience of being turned away is discouraging, nonetheless.

These are students who navigated the labyrinth of college admissions, and who go on to develop techniques in various STEM disciplines to push humanity forward. But in that moment of rejection, they must grapple with a truth that erodes their sense of empowerment and downgrades their care for our political system. The realization is that their voice is muted not by lack of will, but by lack of preparation, and it does not feel good.

This problem is symptomatic of a larger crisis in political know-how. It is after watching this happen for a decade and hearing increasing complaints about our seemingly dysfunctional politics that I decided to take on this topic at length. We are failing our young people by not teaching and talking enough about politics and government. As states reduce civics education and teachers navigate restrictive mandates, the issue only grows more dire. And this is not because children do not want to know these things—the 2023 Harvard Kennedy School's annual youth poll demonstrated an enormous level of interest among young people in becoming involved in politics—it's that they lack the know-how because our systems are failing them.[1]

Right now, we have a very low level of government and political knowledge in the United States, but this also means there's great potential for positive change. Parents can be the ones to start this change by recognizing that imparting the knowledge necessary to become a participating citizen is a parenting responsibility, and one that needs to be taken up by each of us.

In this chapter I lay out just how little our people know about civics, and how harmful that lack of knowledge can be. Acknowledging a problem is the first step to remedying a problem. Let's get started.

What We Don't Know

In 2022, the Annenberg Public Policy Center at the University of Pennsylvania found that fewer than half—just 47% of U.S. adults—could name the three branches of government: executive, legislative, judicial.[2] This knowledge deficit extends to fundamental processes, such as how Congress can override a veto or identifying the Speaker of the House.[3,4]

Surveys that ask about state and local politics yield even more disheartening results. A considerable number of people struggle to name their state representatives or identify their state's governor. Additionally, a significant majority lack knowledge about the legislative processes within their own state.[5]

Assessing political knowledge through national political news questions produces similarly dismal findings. Although there have been only 46 U.S. presidents, a great number of Americans find it challenging to recall a substantial portion of them, including the nation's founders.[6] Furthermore, during presidential election times, a significant portion of the population remains unaware of the vice-presidential candidates.[7]

Though knowing the current Speaker of the House may not be consequential for most people, not knowing even the basics of government is a problem. We have deliberative, legislative bodies who consider our collective issues and offer policies to address these issues at the local, state, and federal level. We have executives such as mayors, governors, and the president who are tasked with executing the laws and leading the multiple government agencies in charge of seeing that our laws are enforced and adhered to. We have a judicial branch responsible for sorting out when individuals or entities either run afoul of the law or use interpretations of the law that force us to reckon with uncertainty or ambiguity with a legal standard. Understanding this fundamental division of power is necessary to conceptualize how the government operates and who makes decisions.

Youth Political Knowledge and Voter Participation

The deficiency in political knowledge is directly linked to lower participation in politics, as evidenced by consistently low voter turnout. Young adults, particularly those between the ages of 18 and 24, have the lowest rates of voter registration and voter turnout.

Nonvoters share some common characteristics that hinder their engagement in the political process. They tend to have limited understanding of the electoral system and lack faith in the impact their vote can make.[8] When asked about the influence of election results on their lives, nonvoters are less likely to perceive any significant impact. Nonvoters often express disinterest in politics, claim a lack of time to gather information, and generally hold less ideological positions on political issues. Some nonvoters who do consume news report feeling discouraged or disconnected from politics, intentionally distancing themselves. Socioeconomic factors, such as lower household incomes and lower satisfaction with personal lives and locations of residence, also contribute to nonvoting patterns. In a 30-year study of youth political participation, not only were recently eligible voters found to be less likely to vote, they were also increasingly less likely to pursue roles as interns for politicians or campaigns.[9]

Some dismiss lower turnout and participation for younger voters as youthful laziness or indifference to politics, but this explanation falls short. Newly eligible voters are often in high school, recent graduates looking to establish themselves in the workforce, or new students starting college. For many of these new adults, navigating the byzantine bureaucracy required to register to vote, finding a polling location or applying for a mail-in ballot, and casting a ballot are simply hard to do for the first time. Recent studies show that young voters are less likely to say they don't care about voting than other age groups and more likely to say the system of voting is too complicated.[10]

Because young people are often mobile—either heading off to college or moving out of the family home to start a life of their own—registering to vote at a new address is typically not a priority, especially if their parents are not regular voters. On top of these logistics-oriented considerations, many young adults come from homes that do not stress the value of participating in politics or that even look down at politics.

Students who transition directly from high school to the workforce have the lowest likelihood of voting, whereas college students vote at significantly higher rates compared to their non-college peers. Several factors contribute to this disparity, including the influence of pursuing higher education and a desire to engage in civic life. Additionally, colleges and universities are increasingly incorporating voting into their student life initiatives.[11]

When people know about a system and how to participate in it, participation goes up. We see this in turnout rates for general elections versus primaries, for presidential years versus midterm years, and for federal races versus local ones. We saw this in 2020 when a record number of people cast mail-in ballots. Voter turnout increased for 18- to 24-year-olds more than it had in decades as the great majority of these new voters were able to vote from home with the guidance of their families during the COVID-19 pandemic.

If our young adults had a bit more instruction around voting, and a better understanding of politics, their participation rates would be greater. What's missing is that parents and families typically don't see this work as a parenting responsibility, and instead think that schools will be able to teach kids all they need to know about how our government works. While schools do have a role in civic instruction, one of the challenges in increasing political know-how and government understanding in schools is that each state gets to set the curricula and instruction time for civics, and in many cases these choices are further delegated to individual school districts. Though there are many benefits to allowing states flexibility in schooling, and though some states teach civics and voter readiness better than others, the overall picture is not promising.

State Variation in Civics Requirements

So, what *does* civics education in the United States look like? It varies from state to state, thanks to our system of federalism whereby states get to make the rules on things such as education. Each state gets to determine how they teach civics—what kind of classes, how long they last, and if there's a test students must pass to graduate high school. Though most high schools have a government or civics requirement, it is often in the last half or quarter of senior year, a time when students are least likely to retain things as they anticipate what's next. In comparison to other subjects, civics often receives the least amount of time per semester in U.S. schools.[12]

While every state has some sort of civics or social studies requirement on the books, what's taught can be a whole different story. As of 2023, there are some states without any mandatory civics classes or tests, others with just a class or a test, and the majority only requiring a semester of civics. Figure 1.1 shows just how much civics education can differ across the country.

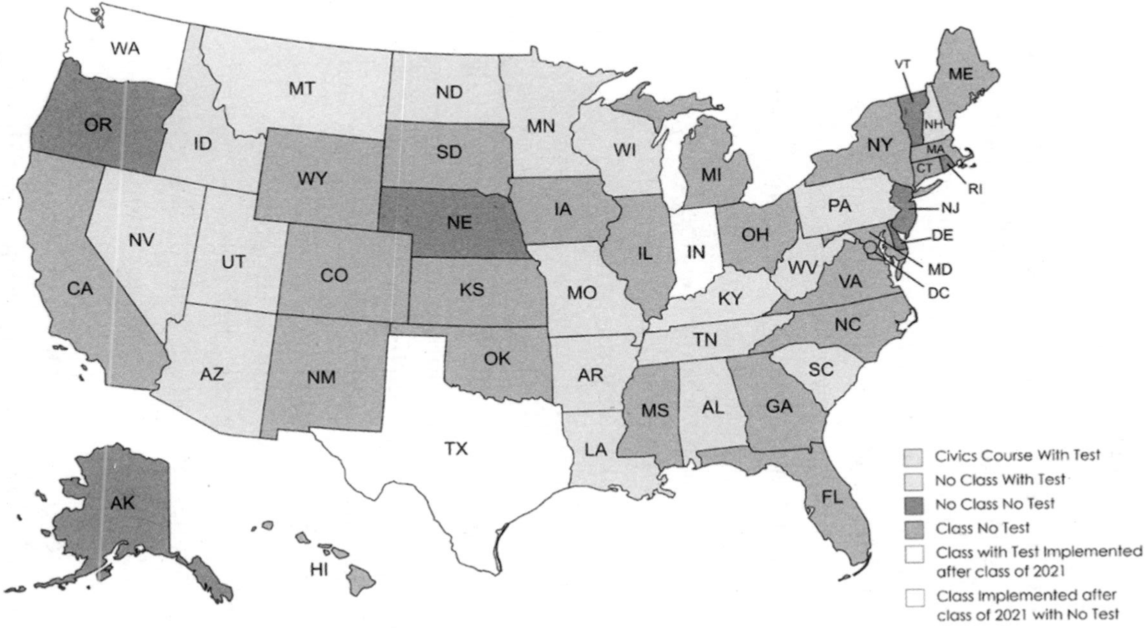
WA
OR
CA
NV
ID
MT
WY
UT
AZ
CO
NM
ND
SD
NE
KS
OK
TX
MN
IA
MO
AR
LA
WI
IL
MI
IN
OH
KY
TN
MS
AL
GA
FL
SC
NC
VA
WV
PA
NY
VT
NH
ME
MA
CT
RI
NJ
DE
MD
DC
AK
HI
Civics Course With Test
No Class With Test
No Class No Test
Class No Test
Class with Test Implemented after class of 2021
Class Implemented after class of 2021 with No Test

Created with mapchart.net

FIGURE 1.1 State civics requirements in the U.S. states.

Kentucky and Montana require students to pass a civics test. Fourteen states mandate a civics course with a test, but only 4 insist on seeing that students pass the test to complete it successfully. Meanwhile, 25 states plus D.C. just have a course, no test needed. Only 9 states and D.C. have a full-year course; and most make do with a semester.

Civics courses usually cover democracy and democratic concepts, the Constitution, and some voting how-to.[13] While no state mandates interaction with local government, some schools get creative with field trips to polling stations or visits with local politicians. Only Maryland and D.C.—both close to the centers of federal governmental power—require community service statewide as a graduation condition. And only 16 states have voter registration forms for use of students in schools.[14]

Within states, the variation of instruction is large. Pennsylvania's got a patchwork approach, with local districts creating their own civics tests, taken any time from seventh to twelfth grade. Idaho starts civics young, integrating it from kindergarten.[15] Colorado demands a year-long civics course to graduate, and to support teachers the Colorado Department of Education developed a set of vocabulary, skills, questions, and content for use in the classroom.[16,17] In New Jersey, where I teach, civics is integrated throughout K–12 social studies, though there's no specific high school requirement.

Of course, it also matters who is assigned to teach civics. Educators acknowledge systemic challenges in staffing civics courses. In researching this book, a team of five research assistants and I interviewed teachers across the nation asking for their insights on the state of civic education. Over the course of our interviews with teachers, we learned a recurring joke, "Everyone at every school knows who has to teach civics, their name is Coach," hinting at the pattern of athletic coaches being assigned to teach civics as a one-off teaching assignment when no one else would do it.

This is not to say there aren't dedicated civics educators working in our schools, there are; it's just that even they often-times find the approach that states and school districts prescribe to be ineffective. Teacher Jen Klein, who has taught civics in Pennsylvania for two decades, shared that the state law does not mandate an actual civics class, but instead that schools can opt to tack on a multiple-choice test like the citizenship exam to a general social studies course to fulfill the requirement. She saw this as detrimental because although kids will cram and pass the test, they do so without directly engaging with topics such as voter registration, contacting elected officials, or understanding the issues addressed at the state and federal levels.

Tom Farrell, an experienced educator in New Jersey, argued that civics should be emphasized more and recommends a sen-ior course with community service to better engage students with local governance, like the programs in Maryland and D.C. He pointed out that while students learn about federal and state governments, they often lack knowledge on local civic involvement.

Lee Hannah, a professor and former high school teacher, explained, "In Virginia, government classes don't have Standards of Learning (SOL) tests, so less effective teachers often teach them to avoid the pressure of high-stakes testing." He suggested that while introducing an SOL might not inherently improve civics education over experiential learning, it could attract more skilled teachers to the subject, as accountability measures often guide teacher assignments.

Though any coach assigned to civics for a semester is undoubtedly doing their best, it's clear that it's hard to deliver content effectively when you've only got a short period of time, and it's outside your own area of expertise. For those dedicated to teaching civics, the work is still hard given that students oftentimes aren't exposed to the material until they are almost through with high school. Our nationwide testing performance shows just how poorly we are doing.

Nationwide Civics Performance: AP U.S. Government and Politics and the National Assessment of Educational Progress

Only a small minority of high school students end up taking AP U.S. Government and Politics. But for the purposes of showing what students know, this is a nationally standardized source of data to consider. In talking with my own students, I've gleaned that those who take it are either interested in government or think it will be an "easy" AP, all with the aim to earn college credit.

The standardized AP Government syllabus is broken into five units:

Foundations of American democracy.

Interactions among branches of government.

Civil liberties and civil rights.

American political ideologies and beliefs.

Political participation.

This is a reasonable set of information to impart to a high school student, though teaching the foundational aspects of the U.S. government in one semester can be challenging. Students would certainly benefit from earlier and longer exposure to concepts like the founding, checks and balances, federalism, civil liberties, civil rights, and political ideologies—but that's simply not the system we have.

AP courses are offered in over 22,000 schools nationwide. A comparison of state high school populations with AP U.S. Government enrollment shows that, unsurprisingly, larger states often have more AP students. However, Washington DC, Maryland, and Virginia have a higher *proportion* of students in AP Government, likely due to their closeness to the federal government. Figure 1.2 presents the number of students enrolled in high school across each state in 2019 as well as the number of students opting into AP Government courses.

The number of students taking the AP U.S. Government exam has increased from 1999 to 2019 in every state, with Virginia having the highest proportion of enrollment in 1999 at just over 2%, and nearly 4% in 2019. Though enrollment is up across all states, some states still have fewer than 1% of students enrolled in the optional course.

Despite growing interest, AP U.S. Government scores suggest the course is not effectively preparing students. It ranks fourth lowest among AP subjects for average scores, with many students not achieving the minimum score of 3 (of the 1–5 AP scale) needed for college credit. Figure 1.3 shows the average AP scores across subjects in 2016 and in 2019 for comparison.

The baseline and movement of these results are both interesting to consider. When compared to the other AP course exams, students in U.S. Government and Politics do quite poorly. From 2016 to 2019, its average score improved slightly, yet remained below 3.

Geographically, there is a wide disparity in how well students perform on this exam. Vermont had the highest average AP Government score at 3.3 in 2019, despite no statewide civics

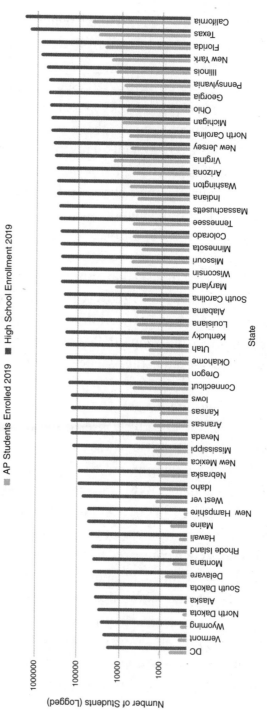

FIGURE 1.2 High school enrollment vs. AP Government enrollment (2019).

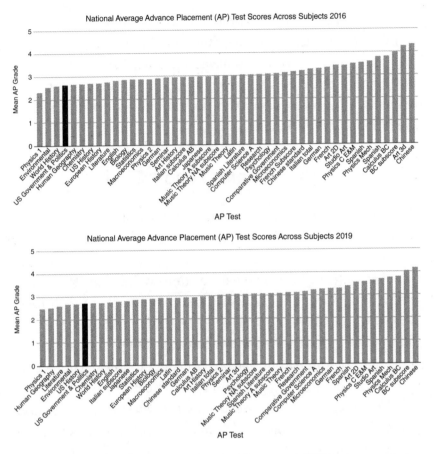

FIGURE 1.3 National average Advance Placement (AP) test scores across subjects (2016 and 2019).

mandate, while New Mexico, with a half-semester civics require-ment, had the lowest at 1.94.

A different approach to comparing AP test performance is to look at the most common score students achieve, known as the modal score. Across states, these statewide modal scores are typically low—1, 2, or 3 out of a possible 5. Notably, in the American South, more students tend to score a 1, which is equiv-alent to having the greatest numbers of all students who decided to take the optional course earn a failing grade.

Considering AP Government is an elective course, typically chosen by motivated students, these results suggest that students not taking the course likely have even lower civics proficiency. Fortunately, there is another method of assessing student civic knowledge for all students, not just those who opt in, known as the Nation's Report Card.

The Nation's Report Card

Beginning in 1988, Congress mandated that the National Center for Education Statistics conduct the National Assessment of Educational Progress (NAEP) survey to report on student achievement in math, science, reading, writing, history, geography, and civics. This assessment survey is called the Nation's Report Card. The test, given to select students in fourth, eighth, and twelfth grades, was last conducted in 2018. In this iteration, only eighth graders took the civics element, now part of a combined "History, Geography, and Civics" section.[18]

The assessment focuses on civic knowledge, dispositions, and skills that encourage civic engagement.[19] Instead of current events trivia, like "Who is the Speaker of the House?" it asks broader questions about citizenship and American principles. It gauges students' attitudes toward democracy and society and evaluates their intellectual skills for engaging in civic life.

From 1998 to 2014, average civics scores for eighth graders rose slightly. But since then, they've plateaued, with most students scoring at or below proficiency: 51% at "basic," 22% "proficient," and 2% "advanced."

The numbers are not promising no matter how we look at them. Young people are not learning enough about politics and government to be invested and involved when they become voting eligible citizens. And beyond just lower voter turnout, there are other downsides to consider.

Impact of Low Civic Know-How—Distrust, Vulnerability to Manipulation, Disempowerment

It's hard to trust something you don't know a lot about. Unsurprisingly, our collective slide in government knowledge also corresponds to a slide in government trust. In 2021, the Pew Research Center asked respondents, "How much of the time do you think you can trust the government in Washington to do what is right?" Only 2% responded "just about always" and just 22% said "most of the time." Since the beginning of the George W. Bush presidency in 2001, our trust in government has declined, though not always in a linear way. These trends do not appear to be due to generational or demographic differences; trust across respondent ages and racial categories has pretty much followed the same basic patterns.

This erosion of trust is concerning, as it highlights the need for a solid understanding of democracy to combat susceptibility to manipulation and misinformation. Without such understanding, people more easily believe outrageous claims about government powers or the actions of politicians. This vulnerability to sensational stories, whether from traditional media or social platforms, undermines our nation's well-being.

Since the 1950s, the American National Election Survey has asked a nationally representative sample of adults about their thoughts on government. One question asks if people believe they have a say in government and another whether the government cares what people think. From 1952–2012, the share of people who thought they could effect change and/or that the government cared for their thoughts at all has dropped. In the most recent years, fewer than 40% of Americans said they had any power to change government and only 18% said the government cared what they thought. These attitudes are pervasive, but they are, for the most part, not correct. And what's worse is that these views, when passed on to our kids, are harmful in the disempowering message that they send.

Not Knowing Creates a Worse Politics

A situation where people are uninformed about how democracy works, don't comprehend the roles of different branches of government, or don't understand their own points of political power leads to a worse politics. It's like sailing a ship without a compass or trying to get through a maze blindfolded. Without knowledge and practice, people can be convinced of a distorted perception of reality and be more prone to accept misguided ideas about the challenges our society faces.

The consequences of this lack of knowledge are far-reaching. When people are easily swayed by sensational stories, media manipulators can exploit this vulnerability, feeding the outrage machine and distracting us from other issues that demand our attention. This sort of despair politics is common today, where rather than having discussions about how we can use our processes for solutions, we find ourselves entangled in a web of distractions and division.

If more of us understood the basics, there would be less room for deception and far better conversations about how to fix the problems we have. A well-informed citizenry is the backbone of a healthy democracy. It enables us to make better decisions, hold our elected officials accountable, and actively participate in shaping our collective destiny. It's something worth working toward as parents.

It's Up to Us to Change

A pervasive lack of knowledge and the related increasing public fatalism have culminated in lower levels of civic participation, voting, knowledge, and political engagement. This has happened in our democratic system—one that is meant to be rooted in power from us, the people. By subcontracting out our care for politics and government to schools, we have allowed ourselves to be both the product and the consumer of educational systems that are not able to do the work of preparing students for the real civic world that we must operate in.

By actively choosing to engage and learn about politics, we can better participate in decision-making processes, advocate for our interests, and contribute to society. By knowing more, we make it more likely our voices are heard, our values are represented, and our concerns are addressed. The payoff of opting in to learn about politics is the ability to actively shape our future and create a more inclusive and responsive democratic system. In passing this on to our kids, we allow them to create a better future for themselves.

We know we have a problematic politics, and that part of the reason things feel so bad is because of how little people know. But how did we get to this place? It is worth exploring *why* a significant number of people lack a deep understanding of civics and the workings of government. That is the focus of the next chapter.

Notes

1. Harvard Kennedy School Institute of Politics. (2023). Survey of Young Americans' Attitudes Toward Politics and Public Service, 45th Edition (13–22 March).
2. Annenberg Public Policy Center. (2022). Americans' civics knowledge drops on First Amendment and branches of government (13 September).
3. Annenberg Public Policy Center (2014). Americans know surprisingly little about their government, survey finds.
4. Delli Carpini, M.X. and Keeter, S. (1996). *What Americans Know About Politics and Why It Matters*. New Haven, CT: Yale University Press; Delli Carpini, M.X. and Keeter, S. (1992). The public's knowledge of politics. In: *Public Opinion, the Press, and Public Policy* (ed. J.D. Kennamer), 19–40. Westport, CT: Praeger.

5. Rosen, J. (2018). Americans don't know much about state government, survey finds. The Hub; Mettler, S. (2011). *The Submerged State: How Invisible Government Policies Undermine American Democracy*. Chicago: University of Chicago Press.

6. The U.S. Mint. (2007). Survey reveals most Americans can't name nation's Founding Fathers (15 August). https://www.usmint.gov/news/press-releases/20070815-survey-reveals-most-americans-cant-name-nations-founding-fathers.

7. Rossoll, N. (2016). More than 40 percent of Americans cannot name VP candidates. *ABC News* (2 October).

8. Amandi, F., Williams, A., Feldman, D., et al. (2020). The 100 million project: The untold story of American non-voters. The Knight Foundation.

9. Syvertsen, A.K., Wray-Lake, L. Flanagan, C.A., et al. (2011). Thirty-year trends in US adolescents' civic engagement: A story of changing participation and educational differences. *Journal of Research on Adolescence 21* (3): 586–594.

10. Amandi et al., The 100 million project.

11. Whitley, C.T. and Yoder, S.D. (2015). Developing social responsibility and political engagement: Assessing the aggregate impacts of university civic engagement on associated attitudes and behaviors. *Education, Citizenship and Social Justice 10* (3): 217–233.

12. Shapiro, S. and Brown, C. (2018). Report: The state of civics education. The Center for American Progress (21 February). https://www.americanprogress.org/article/state-civics-education/.

13. Shapiro and Brown, The state of civics education.

14. Center for Information & Research on Civic Learning & Engagement. (2023). State policies and statutes that support growing voters (15 September). https://circle.tufts.edu/latest-research/state-statutes-support-growing-voters.

15. Idaho Department of Education. (2016).

16. Colorado Department of Education. (2018). Graduation guidelines, https://www.cde.state.co.us/postsecondary/graduationguidelines.

17. Shapiro, S. and Brown, C. (2018). A look at civics education in the United States. *American Educator 42* (2): 10.

18. The sampling selection criteria for the schools used to take the exam are designed to ensure that different types are represented: small and big; urban, suburban, and rural locations; public and private schools. Within selected schools, students are randomly selected and then randomly assigned to one of two possible exams administered in each wave. Individual scores are not reported; rather, the data is weighted to account for relative frequency of student demographics (race, sex, ethnicity) in an attempt to get a big-picture view on what U.S. students of all different backgrounds know and how that knowledge is or is not related to the type of school and setting.

19. National Assessment Governing Board. (2018).

2

Routes to Our Civic Deficit

If you've decided to read this book, it's likely because you feel that something is off in the way our politics operates. We're all swimming in a sea of information and content, yet when it comes to civic know-how, it feels like we're just treading water. In the last chapter, I described how little we know. In this chapter, I work through four major reasons we find ourselves in this civic deficit. As a preview, here are the basic reasons many of us feel like we don't know as much about politics as we should:

- **Intricate by Design:** The U.S. political system has layers, checks, balances, and a fair share of complexity.

- **A Tradition of Not Talking:** For too long, politics has been the elephant in the room that we've been told not to talk about.

- **Hating Politics:** When we do talk about politics, we don't employ strategies that inspire more engagement.

- **School's Out:** We often pass the teaching baton to schools, but the reality is they aren't up to this task for a variety of reasons. Parents are part of this story.

I spend the most time in the chapter on the final point. Though the first three reasons are important to understand, part of the underlying premise of this book is that it's up to parents to do the work of raising a citizen. Why is it up to parents? Well, because schools—where most of us believe our children will learn the necessary things about being a citizen and how to understand and work within our government—are not really capable of imparting the necessary lessons. To fix a problem, you must name it, and understand how it became a problem in the first place, and then work on solutions. In this chapter, I go over how we find ourselves in this low civic know-how predicament and why schools won't be the way out.

Intricate by Design: The U.S. System Can Be Tough to Understand

Though the U.S. system is held up as an example of a functioning democracy,[1] it's by no means an easy system to understand and participate in. We have a complex structure of checks and balances making it hard to understand decision-making processes. If you print the Constitution on standard size paper using a 12-point font, you'd have to read 19 pages of rules to figure out how just the federal system works. Though 19 pages might not seem like a lot, most Americans have never read it,[2] and those who have tend to forget many parts.[3]

When it comes to knowing how to participate, each state is individually responsible for administering elections, and other than for big federal elections such as the presidency and Congress, most elections happen on different years and days across different states for all different levels of government. For instance, in 2023 for the local position of mayor, 507 different localities voted to select their mayors across 37 states (the other 13 states hold elections for mayors in different years), on 30 different dates ranging from the earliest mayoral election in Enid, Oklahoma (pop. 50,566) on February 14, 2023, to Culver City, California (pop. 39,970) on December 12, 2023.[4] This is all to say, the system has a lot going on, which can feel like a lot to keep track of.

Additionally, the behemoth of the two-party system can be daunting for people to understand. The binary structure of Democrats versus Republicans often leads to a choice that does not capture the full spectrum of political beliefs. What's more, at the state and local level a larger array of political organizations comes into play, making the "real" contest in an election happen at the earlier primary stage, in a way that only very involved partisans might fully grasp. All of this is understandably frustrating, but none of it must be.

One of the reasons we don't know as much about politics and government as we want to is that it truly takes time and effort to understand it. Any adult navigating all the challenges of life is certainly equipped to better understand our system, but it's not surprising that without a push, many people don't.

The "Shh" Tradition: Not Talking About Politics

Many parents of today had parents who never talked to them about politics; it's no wonder that we don't know how to talk about these topics with our own kids.

Politics has long been a conversational no-go in the United States, guided by nineteenth-century etiquette norms that discouraged imposing one's political views on others. These norms, documented in pamphlets and books of the era, have been passed down generationally.[5] As a further limiter, for most of our history political discourse has remained in the realm of men, with very few spaces for women or children to voice their opinions publicly. Later etiquette texts discouraged criticism of politicians, particularly in their presence.[6] Another standard bit of advice was to *know where you stand* and retain a fixed political opinion lest other conversationalists find you to be less than a gentleman or lady of the time.[7] The idea was that nuance and a give-and-take would signal a thoughtless or unserious attempt rather than engaged consideration more becoming of thinking people.

By the 1980s, etiquette writers admitted that politics can be an acceptable topic of conversation, provided that the conversation was handled correctly. Judith Martin, the author of *Miss Manners' Guide for the Turn-of-the-Millennium*, gave this advice in 1989: "Grilling people and insulting their beliefs are rude. But using the occasion of an election to talk about how the country should be run, or who is qualified to do it, can produce acceptable stimulating conversation."[8]

Today, a plethora of news source opinion pieces, parent blog articles, and magazine advice columns advise against talking politics with or in front of children. Some warn that because of their young age children are "not equipped to process [politics] emotionally or intellectually" and caution parents against discussing politics for fear of giving their children "anxiety-inducing information they're not ready to understand."[9] Others argue that because children can feel our own anxiety about politics when we talk in front of them, we ought not do so in their presence.[10]

There of course are people and organizations that see this differently—as I do—working to encourage intergenerational political discourse, but these voices are new and still in the minority.

Hating Politics: Talking About Politics in a Negative Way

Children are sensitive observers, attuned to the attitudes and conversations of the adults around them. When these young minds hear grown-ups openly saying things like, "All politicians are corrupt!" or "I hate President Obama!" or "President Trump is a liar!" children begin to associate politics with something ugly and the people involved as villains rather than potential role models. This kind of repeated negative exposure can plant the seeds of cynicism in children's minds, working to grow a view that politics is inherently divisive and those involved in it are untrustworthy.

For many parents, feelings of political distrust are undeniable. However, airing only frustrated opinions primes children to dislike politics and government from a very early age. When negativity becomes the dominant narrative, it sets the stage for children to develop an aversion to the very processes that shape their society. Our media coverage does enough in promoting outrage around politics; we don't need to do the same in our homes.

School's Out: Why Our Schools Can't Do This Work

We ask a lot of the teachers in our educational systems. There have been calls for schools to step up and offer detailed instruction on how to vote, aiming to bridge the gap in civic education.[11] I truly believe the vast majority of people working in schools want what's best for children, but they, like everyone else, face constraints on what they can deliver. To assess why schools aren't up for this task, I and a team of research assistants interviewed over 50 teachers, compiled a state-by-state look at civics' requirements, reviewed historical curricular and testing trends, analyzed large sets of data on AP U.S. Government and other nationalized civics tests, and traced the lineage of legal cases challenging the introduction of political or government topics in the classroom. The curricular differences and test scores are described in the previous chapter. Scores show the state of our civic education, but talking with teachers and working through the recent history of schooling gave us the clearest views into the evolving classroom dynamics and the challenges faced in imparting civic knowledge.

The teachers we interviewed pushed us to investigate different facets of modern schooling that make it difficult to teach civics in a more robust way. Two major culprits bear the blame, though there are many forces at play. First, there's the relentless prioritization of subjects assessed for standardized tests, which overshadows and crowds out class time for civic awareness lessons. Second, a fear of parental agitation with the associated specter of negative media coverage and even potential lawsuits grips the minds of school administrators and teachers.

A Short History of Public Schools and Civic Orientation

Since its early settlements, the United States modeled its schools after European systems, aiming not just to impart basic skills like reading and math, but also to prepare students—at least those from upper echelons of society—for public life.[12] In the late 1700s, colonial "common schools" offered education for a fee to children of various ages.[13] These schools, seen as pillars to the republic's growth, allowed parents to negotiate with teachers about the curriculum and costs, all with an understanding about the importance of education to grow the fledgling nation's prosperity.

After the Revolutionary War (1775–1783), the United States gradually embraced the concept public education. State-funded public schools emerged in the 1830s and 1840s, with all states having at least one public school in place by 1870.[14] During this time, politician, bureaucrat, and educational reformer Horace Mann was pivotal in shaping American education, advocating for state-supported public schools to cultivate more informed and responsible citizens.[15,16] It is from his work that governments began to allocate tax revenue to support the widespread establishment of schools for children to attend.

The teaching profession, initially male-dominated, shifted as the "Republican motherhood" ideology gained traction, emphasizing the duty of women to nurture virtuous citizens. This shift led to more educational opportunities for women and eventually to a predominantly female teaching workforce. Today, 75% of elementary school teachers, 60% of middle school teachers, and close to 50% of high school teachers are women.[17]

During the late 1800s to the mid-1900s, local school systems were often controlled by politicians who leveraged their power to advance their political agendas.[18] This involved providing jobs to their supporters and ensuring that schools were available for the children of constituencies they considered necessary for their political success. One notable figure during this period was John Dewey, an educational reformer based in Chicago and New York City. Dewey believed that education played a necessary role in promoting democracy, even though he was not a proponent of the existing public school system.[19] According to Dewey, schools should serve a higher purpose than merely equipping children with workforce skills. He emphasized that schools should be places where children learn how to lead fulfilling lives, benefiting both themselves and society. Booker T. Washington shared many of Dewey's views and argued for similar styles of reform within Black political and educational circles. He advocated for integrated schools that would prepare students for more than just working in segregated industries.[20]

Over time, the United States witnessed an expansion of schooling and the role for public education in promoting civic know-how, but in the twentieth century the country experienced pivotal shifts in testing, education policy, and landmark court cases that have collectively influenced the current approach to civics education, contributing to its decline in schools.

The Rise of Standardized Tests and Curricular Crowd Out

As the notion of childhood education grew from primary, to secondary, to post-secondary higher education, concerns about standardizing curricula and admission processes led educators and administrators, both in private and public settings, to adopt exams as a convenient metric for student assessment. While the rise of standardized testing did not diminish the focus on civic instruction right away, the emphasis on such testing worked to subtly shift educational priorities, culminating in the test-focused instruction prevalent in today's high schools.

In 1900, the College Entrance Examination Board was created to standardize New England boarding school instruction. By 1901, essay exams assessed student proficiency in areas like Latin and physics.[21] Meanwhile, compulsory education laws were enacted nationwide, mandating elementary education through the age of 14 by 1930.[22]

In World War I, there was a desire to routinize the way military officers were selected, which led to the development of IQ tests. Harvard's Robert Yerkes, drawing on Frenchman Alfred Binet's psychological work, created such tests, impacting military and civilian assessment methods alike.[23] Despite criticism at the time, the concept of using exams to rank individuals stuck and was adopted by the military into the Armed Services Vocational Aptitude Battery, which is still in use today. The test-and-rank approach influenced various standardized tests shaping educational assessment for generations.

In the 1920s, Carl Brigham, a Princeton psychologist and known eugenicist, created the SAT to assess intelligence.[24] Launched in 1926, the SAT's multiple-choice format was a departure from prior essay-based exams, covering a range of topics from vocabulary to logic.[25] Initially, its use was limited to a few East Coast schools but by the 1930s, the SAT became a staple of Ivy League admissions, and other institutions used it for scholarship considerations. At the same time, standardized testing filtered down to public schools, where schools began to standardize curricula to produce students who would receive higher marks on exams.[26]

By 1940, half of the young adults in the U.S. population had completed high school.[27] By the 1950s, the Cold War prompted federal interest in education reform, with a new emphasis on science, math, engineering, and technology to bolster the nation's global standing.[28] With only so many instructional hours in a day, some subjects had to be deprioritized to afford space for these subjects. At the same time, standardized testing expanded and evolved. The SAT, by then managed by the Educational Testing Service, adapted to include sections like reading comprehension and analogies, and was administered to half a million students annually by the end of the decade. In 1959, the ACT was introduced as an alternative to the SAT. Created by education professor Everett Franklin Lindquist, the ACT was designed to evaluate high school knowledge in English, math, social studies, and natural sciences, focusing more on learned academic content than the SAT's abstract skill assessment.[29] Since then, both the SAT and ACT have been used as one of the key indicators colleges consider when selecting incoming students.

After a few decades of the increased use of standardized tests, civics education saw a decline. From 1928 to 1972, there was a 40% drop in ninth-grade civics course enrollment.[30]

In 1975, a notable decrease in SAT scores nationwide drew the attention of lawmakers. The 1983 report "A Nation at Risk: The Imperative for Educational Reform" by the National Commission on Excellence in Education claimed American education was underperforming, endangering the nation's future competitiveness. It went so far as to suggest that if an "unfriendly foreign power had imposed the mediocre educational performance that exists today on America, we might have considered it an act of war."[31] While the report recognized the importance of an educated citizenry for a thriving democracy, it placed greater emphasis on promoting literacy and labor market skills rather than civic knowledge and preparation. The report sparked debate about its implications for democracy, drawing criticism for sidelining teachers' perspectives,[32] and attempting to produce students prepared to work for corporations, rather than developing the skills needed to critique and actively participate in government.[33] Post-report, many U.S. schools changed course, often at the expense of civics classes.

Like any connected system, the feedback mechanisms in schooling and testing impact one another. By 1989, the ACT replaced its Social Studies and Natural Sciences sections with Science Reasoning and Reading, for closer comparison with the SAT. This shift away from assessing social studies, history, and civics knowledge coincided with a generation of parents today who were educated during a time when such topics were deemphasized in schools. It's no surprise that many of our parents, and ourselves, feel less knowledgeable about government and politics than we'd like to be—we were educated in a system that did not prioritize these subjects.

Pushing Civics out of Schools: Testing Today

Civics education is often sidelined in U.S. schools, due to curricular crowd-out in the pursuit of high standardized test scores—none of which include civics. Ben Lewis, a Texas middle school teacher, echoed many educators' concerns that the preoccupation with tests has pushed social studies aside. With schools focusing on math and reading intensely in middle school, high school educators struggle to fill the civics education gap with incoming students who have never been exposed to basic governmental concepts. Dana Davenport, an AP U.S. Government teacher in California, noted in her interview that while school boards may try to influence curriculum standards in favor of more civics, the lack of civics in standardized tests leads to little enforcement of civics education benchmarks.

The 2002 No Child Left Behind (NCLB) law, with its emphasis on math, reading, and science, has further caused a reduction in social studies time. A broader 2018 survey revealed that many teachers, especially those of younger students, find civics education time insufficient, often overshadowed by subjects included in standardized testing.[34] When asked which subjects teachers chose to reduce to meet the NCLB targets, most mentioned social studies.[35] The teachers also highlighted a lack of resources and the potential controversy of civics topics as barriers. These findings echo the experiences of my first-year students, who report a neglect of civics in high school due to its absence from SAT or ACT score considerations, and a reluctance to tackle controversial issues.

Our educational system, both public and private, places a high emphasis on test performance, using SAT and ACT scores and college admission rates as key metrics for success rather than focusing on the rate of preparing engaged citizens.[36] This has led to a widespread practice of "teaching to the test." Despite teachers recognizing the downsides of "teaching to the test," the pressure from parents and administrators for high test scores means educators often have little choice but to adopt this approach.

It's not just that teaching to the test works, or that is easier, or that it insulates teachers and administrators from potential parental ire; it also makes economic sense for schools to do it.

Schools with top test scores often attract affluent families, creating a cycle where a school's prestige is intertwined with community wealth, which in turn helps a school by having more parent money to support school initiatives. Another significant factor driving the emphasis on test scores is the influence of state and federal funding, and sometimes private grants. When allocating educational funds, especially under budget constraints, legislators tend to rely on easily quantifiable outcomes like test scores for making funding decisions, including school grant awards and when making choices on which schools to close. Consequently, school administrators and teachers, under pressure from parents and decreasing public support in many areas, often find themselves incentivized to focus on test preparation above civic readiness.

Pushing Civics out of Schools: A Century of Challenges in the Courts

In the twentieth century, in addition to the rise of standardized testing, the role of schools in promoting patriotism and civic engagement faced legal scrutiny. Early challenges to school practices of patriotic acts failed, but over time, shifts in the judiciary and their interpretations of the Constitution resulted in a notable decrease in the schools' civic mandate.

As public schooling became universal, schools were tasked with instilling patriotic values through practices like the flag salute, which began during WWI, and the recitation of the Pledge of Allegiance as a morning ritual.[37] Advocates argued that such practices were necessary to shore up national identity and democratic values. Critics contended that compulsory participation infringed on individual rights, equating it to forced patriotism, which was counter to the freedom of expression protected in the First Amendment to the Constitution.

A landmark case involved Jehovah's Witness students Lillian and William Gobitis, who in the late 1930s refused to salute the flag in school, citing their religious beliefs, which held that their allegiance should be solely dedicated to God's Kingdom and that pledging allegiance to any other government would contradict that commitment. Their expulsion and subsequent lawsuit led to the Supreme Court case *Minersville School District v. Gobitis*. In 1940, the Court upheld the school's policy in an 8–1 decision, prioritizing patriotism over religious freedoms.

A few years after the *Gobitis* case, the Supreme Court addressed a similar situation originating in West Virginia, where Jehovah's Witness students also refused to salute the flag. On Flag Day in 1943, in *West Virginia State Board of Education v. Barnette*, the Court reversed its stance in a 6–3 decision, ruling that the First Amendment protected the students' right to abstain from the flag salute, emphasizing that peaceful dissent is a constitutional right.

The *Barnette* ruling didn't immediately end mandatory flag salutes in schools, but it started a gradual change. In 1966, New Jersey's Supreme Court dealt with a similar issue in *Holden v. Elizabeth Board of Education*, where Muslim students were suspended for not saluting the flag. The court again upheld their right to abstain, reflecting the *Barnette* decision. The Pledge of Allegiance, particularly its phrase "under God," which was added in 1954 to contrast with the Soviet Union's atheism, has also been legally contested.[38] The case *Lipp v. Morris* in 1978 saw a New Jersey student challenge mandatory participation in the Pledge, resulting in a ruling that such state mandates infringe on First Amendment rights.

Despite these rulings, enforcement has always been in consistent due to a mix of ignorance of legal standards and defiance by some schools.[39] This led to the continuation of flag salutes in many schools across the United States, often unchallenged, and thus becoming a routine part of school life perhaps even for you—it was for me in the 1990s in Kansas. Today, while 47 states have statutes regarding the Pledge of Allegiance or flag salutes, they all now include provisions allowing students to opt out.[40]

Beyond displays of patriotism, courts have considered what it means for schools to be places of political activity. During the Vietnam War, courts upheld students' rights to political expression in school. Perhaps the most notable Supreme Court decision on the subject was *Tinker v. Des Moines* (1969), where students won the right to wear armbands protesting the war, as the school could not prove their actions disrupted operations.

Teachers' political rights have also been addressed by the courts. In *Sterzing v. Fort Bend ISD* (1972), a teacher won his case after being dismissed for expressing views on interracial marriage in class. The court ruled his First Amendment rights were violated and established guidelines for teachers discussing sensitive topics, balancing the need for objectivity with community standards.[41] In 1976, teacher Dean Wilson faced controversy for inviting communist speaker Anton Kchmareck to his political science class, having previously hosted speakers from various political parties and backgrounds without issue. Following protocol, he obtained approval from the principal and school board. However, after public outcry, the school board banned "all political speakers" from Molalla Union High School. Wilson and a student's mother sued, claiming the ban violated the First and Fourteenth Amendments. A federal judge ruled the ban unreasonable, highlighting no prior disruptions and no harm to educational goals. The judge clarified the judiciary's role wasn't to set curricula but emphasized that such a ban unreasonably limited free speech and failed the school's educational duty in civic education.[42]

These rulings established important guidelines for teachers when discussing civic topics, but as with the earlier decisions on flag salutes and the Pledge, many teachers operate within systems under local control, and without strict adherence to what courts have decided in the past. Though they may have a right to talk about certain political topics, the reality is that under pressures from administrators not to upset parents, many find it easier to avoid the subject all together.

In 1996, the California Teachers Association challenged San Diego Unified School District's ban on political buttons at work, leading to a complex legal battle. Courts eventually ruled that while teachers could be restricted from political expression during instructional time in the classroom, they retained the right to express political views during nonteaching periods on school grounds.[43] Meaning that teachers have a right to be political, but owing to their authority in a classroom, it's considered inappropriate for those politics to be on display to students.

While teachers have latitude in how they deliver material, they are subject to control at the administrator level, like other state employees. A significant case that influenced the approach to teacher speech originated outside of schools. The 2006 Supreme Court case of *Garcetti v. Ceballos* came about when Richard Ceballos, a district attorney, was denied a promotion allegedly for criticizing a warrant. The Court decided that public employees' speech is not protected under the First Amendment when made as part of official duties. This ruling, while not specific to education, clarified that teachers, like other state employees, have limitations on political speech during their professional responsibilities. The Court held that a public employee's speech is protected only when it is expressed as a private citizen, not as part of their official duties, consistent with the earlier decision in the San Diego Unified School District.[44]

A case similar to *Garcetti v. Ceballos* arose in the public school setting with *Mayer v. Monroe County Community School Corporation* (2007). In this case, teacher Deborah Mayer argued her First Amendment rights were violated when her contract wasn't renewed after discussing a political protest during class. A student asked Mayer about her own participation in a protest action, and she acknowledged honking for a "Honk for Peace" sign. Parents complained that she talked about this, and her principal then barred political stances in class. Mayer saw this as the reason for her contract's nonrenewal, which was the reason she sued her school system.

The Seventh Circuit referenced *Garcetti v. Ceballos*, ruling Mayer's speech as a public employee did not have First Amendment protection. Her contract nonrenewal was upheld, suggesting teachers' political expressions in class are limited. This case has influenced the cautious approach educators now take toward political discussions in the classroom.

The cases discussed here provide a context for understanding why teachers and schools are not eager to engage in robust political instruction. The legal journey through the intersection of education and politics has left teachers and administrators in a bit of a bind, where it's just riskier to talk about politics, and on top of the pressures of curricular crowd-out, it's no wonder schools aren't the sites of civic education they could be.

Pushing Civics out of Schools:
Parental Blowback

Another reason our schools shy away from civics education is due to the fear of parental backlash or lawsuits. While only a few complaints escalate to legal action, even informal parental grievances can pressure schools to alter their curricula to prevent potential legal battles or negative media attention.

Controversies in school instruction around politics receive considerable media attention, with reports over the last 30 years on topics like the Vietnam War,[45] abortion,[46] 9/11,[47] gender identity,[48] sexuality,[49,50] and international events such as the Paris attacks of 2015[51] and the 2023 Israel–Palestine conflict.[52] This media spotlight, as well as the complexity of many political subjects, makes educators wary of engaging in such discussions.

Talking about politics carries more risks compared to teaching subjects like trigonometry or English grammar. Administrators in recent years have grappled with how to teach U.S. government and history amidst accusations of bias and the politicization of racial history education.[53] The pandemic exacerbated these challenges, with teachers modifying or avoiding controversial topics in virtual classrooms to prevent parental backlash, according to a number of the teachers we interviewed in the summer of 2020. Even calls for federal oversight of school curricula have emerged from Congress, despite education traditionally being a state and local responsibility.[54]

Conclusion

The intricacies of the U.S. political system, with its many layers and mechanisms, present a challenge for any educational framework—especially one that must be delivered during just one semester in high school. Our societal strategy of not talking about politics or getting frustrated as the default and primary reaction aren't helping the situation.

While many of us look to schools to shoulder the responsibility of teaching civics, it's clear that they face numerous obstacles that hinder their ability to do this effectively. It's not just an institutional issue; as parents and community members, we're part of this narrative too. Teacher Ben Lewis, like others, pointed to two big things that would make our civics instruction better: spreading civics education over the school years, rather than condensing it into a short course, and including more about local elections. School curricula are unlikely to expand, but luckily, we as parents do have a longer time with our children to introduce and review parts about the government and politics throughout childhood. We also have more flexibility to focus on local and state government, in a way that can augment lessons in schools.

None of this is meant to say that schools and teachers aren't trying. They are, and many have multi-semester-long option programs like the renowned *We the People: The Citizen and the Constitution* program. I have this program and teachers like Ken Thomas to thank for inspiring me to pursue the route that I have. Being able to attend a school that provided this sort of program is an exception, not the norm.

What's clear is that teachers know students aren't learning enough about civics. In my experience, I too see that students don't know enough by the time they are eligible to participate. With school constraints, the role of parents in civics education at home becomes necessary. And in the following chapters I'll describe why it's good for you to take on this task, and how to do it.

Notes

1. Though the U.S. score in *Freedom in the World*, an index maintained by freedomhouse.org, fell by 11 points on a 100-point scale in the decade from 2010 to 2020—see Freedom in the World 2022: Reversing the Decline of Democracy in the United States by Sarah Repucci.

2. Marquette Law School. (2019). Marquette Law School Supreme Court Survey. https://law.marquette.edu/poll/wp-content/uploads/2019/10/MULawSC2019Toplines.pdf.

3. CBS News. (2021). Most Americans don't know what's in the Constitution: "A crisis of civic education." CBS Mornings (19 January. https://www.cbsnews.com/news/constitution-americans-civics-test/.

4. The United States Conference of Mayors. 2023 Mayoral Election Calendar and Results. https://www.usmayors.org/elections/election-results-2/.

5. Martine, A. (1866). *Martine's Hand-Book of Etiquette, and Guide to True Politeness*.

6. Martine, *Martine's Hand-Book of Etiquette, and Guide to True Politeness*.

7. Hartley, F. (1860). *The Ladie's Book of Etiquette, and Manual of Politeness*.

8. Martin, J. (1989). Miss Manners on office etiquette. *Fortune 120* (11): 155.

9. Margolis, R. (2018). Stop talking to your kids about politics. The Week (19 November). https://theweek.com/articles/807702/stop-talking-kids-about-politics.

10. Green, E. (2020). How to keep your kids out of the culture war. *The Atlantic* (22 November). https://www.theatlantic.com/politics/archive/2020/11/how-talk-kids-children-politics-election/617169/.

11. Holbein, J.B. and Hillygus, D.S. (2020). *Making Young Voters: Converting Civic Attitudes into Civic Action*. New York: Cambridge University Press.

12. Throughout our history, the connection between citizenship and education has remained strong despite significant changes in our school systems and institutions. While this section focuses on more recent developments in schooling, there is a vast body of literature exploring the history of civics in U.S. schools for those interested in reading more on the matter. See: Kaestle, C.F. (1983). *Pillars of the Republic: Common Schools and American Society, 1780–1860* (vol. 154). New York: Macmillan; Katz, M.S. (1976). A History of Compulsory Education Laws. Fastback Series, No. 75. Bicentennial Series; Moss, D.A. (2017). The struggle over public education in early America (1851). In: *Democracy*, 208–243. Cambridge, MA: Harvard University Press; Beatty, B. (1995). *Preschool Education in America: The Culture of Young Children from the Colonial Era to the Present*. New Haven, CT: Yale University Press; Hinman, B. (2012). The scoop on school and work in Colonial America. Capstone Classroom.

13. Kaestle, *Pillars of the Republic.*

14. Tyack, D. and Hansot, E. (1992). *Learning Together: A History of Coeducation in American Public Schools.* New York: Russell Sage Foundation; Hirst, J.D. (1991). Public health and the public elementary schools, 1870–1907. *History of Education* 20 (2): 107–118. During this period, access to elite education remained limited to the wealthy, who either sent their children to preparatory schools in Europe or hired private tutors.

15. Messerli, J. and Lloyd, T. (1972). *Horace Mann: A Biography.* New York: Knopf; Mondale, S. (Ed.). (2002). *School: The Story of American Public Education.* Boston: Beacon Press

16. Mann's advocacy, while hailed as a positive influence on the development of public schooling in the United States, reflected the racial and gender biases of his era. His vision for "universal school" meant school for white boys and certain immigrants, pushing nonwhite children to a version of segregated, vocational education.

17. Ingersoll, R.M., Merrill, E., Stuckey, D., and Collins, G. (2018). Seven trends: The transformation of the teaching force – Updated October 2018. CPRE Research Reports.

18. Hooser, A. and McClain, J. (2022). Introduction to the teaching profession. In: *EESE 2010 Introduction to Education.* Murfreesboro, TN: Middle Tennessee State University.

19. Benson, L., Harkavy, I.R., and Puckett, J.L. (2007). *Dewey's Dream: Universities and Democracies in an Age of Education Reform: Civil Society, Public Schools, and Democratic Citizenship.* Philadelphia: Temple University Press.

20. Moore, J.M. (2003). *Booker T. Washington, W.E.B. Du Bois, and the Struggle for Racial Uplift* (Vol. 1). Wilmington, DE: SR Books.

21. Fuess, C.M. (1950). *The College Board.* New York: Columbia University Press.

22. Richardson, J.G. (1980). Variation in date of enactment of compulsory school attendance laws: An empirical inquiry. *Sociology of Education*: 153–163.

23. Today, modified versions of Binet's test are still administered, mainly for admissions to selective kindergarten programs.

24. Zwick, R. (2022). A century of testing controversies. In: *The History of Educational Measurement: Key Advancements in Theory, Policy, and Practice* (ed. B.E. Clauser and M.B. Bunch), 136–154. New York: Routledge.

25. Lemann, N. (2000). *The Big Test: The Secret History of the American Meritocracy.* New York: Macmillan.

26. Cuban, L. (1984). *How Teachers Taught: Constancy and Change in American Classrooms, 1890–1980.* Research on Teaching Monograph Series. New York: Teachers College Press.

27. Herbst, J. (2004). *The Once and Future School: Three Hundred and Fifty Years of American Secondary Education.* New York: Routledge.

28. Rudolph, J. (2002). *Scientists in the Classroom: The Cold War Reconstruction of American Science Education*. New York: Springer.
29. Kamenetz, A. (2015). *The Test: Why Our Schools Are Obsessed with Standardized Testing–But You Don't Have to Be*. New York: Public Affairs.
30. Niemi, R.G. and Smith. J. (2001). Enrollments in high school government classes: Are we short-changing both citizenship and political science training? *PS: Political Science & Politics 34* (2): 281–287.
31. National Commission on Excellence in Education. (1983). A nation at risk: The imperative for educational reform. *The Elementary School Journal 84* (2): 113–130.
32. Hunt, J.W. (2008). A nation at risk and no child left behind: Déja vu for administrators? *Phi Delta Kappan 89* (8): 580–585.
33. Evans, R.W. (2014). *Schooling Corporate Citizens: How Accountability Reform Has Damaged Civic Education and Undermined Democracy*. New York: Routledge.
34. Kurtz, H., Lloyd, S., Harwin, A., and Osher, M. (2018). Civics education in K-12 schools. Results of a national survey. Editorial Projects in Education.
35. Kahne, J. and Middaugh, E. (2008). High quality civic education: What is it and who gets it? *Social Education 72* (1): 34.
36. Evans, B.J. (2015). College admission testing in America. In: *International Perspectives in Higher Education Admission Policy: A Reader* (ed. V. Stead), 173–179. New York: Peter Lang.
37. Coutts, M.T. (1942). How the flag pledge originated. *Journal of Education 125* (7): 225–226.
38. Pub.L. 83-396, Chap. 297, 68 Stat. 249, H.J.Res. 243, enacted 14 June 1954.
39. Gaffney, P.V. and Gaffney, F.M. (1996). Analysis of and educators' attitudes toward the right of public school students regarding mandatory participation in patriotic school exercises. ERIC ED398217.
40. Dress, B. (2022). Here is a breakdown of laws in 47 states that require reciting the Pledge of Allegiance. *The Hill* (2 April). https://thehill.com/homenews/3256719-47-states-require-the-pledge-of-allegiance-be-recited-in-schools-here-is-a-breakdown-of-each-states-laws/.
41. Sterzing retired from teaching rather than being reinstated and went on to be a financial planner until his death in 2017.
42. *Wilson V. Chancellor* Civ. No. 76-92 418 F.Supp. 1358. (1976). United States District Judge, James Milton Burns of the United States District Court for the District of Oregon.
43. *California Teachers Association v. Governing Board of San Diego Unified School District*. Court of Appeal, Fourth District, Division 1, California No. D020372 (1996).
44. *Garcetti v. Ceballos* DOCKET NO. 04-473 U.S. Supreme Court (2006).

45. Seo, D. (1995). Getting Vietnam War into classrooms is still a battle. *Los Angeles Times* (1 May).

46. Doig, M. (2002). Pamphlet plan angers parents; 35 of them complain about an effort to pass out anti-abortion material in schools. *Sarasota Herald Tribune* (12 April).

47. San Antonio Express-News Staff. (2004). "Fahrenheit 9-11" viewing at high school upsets parent; English teacher showed the documentary condemning Bush. *San Antonio Express-News* (10 October).

48. Starnes, T. (2015). Parents furious over school's plan to teach gender spectrum, fluidity. Fox News (16 May). https://www.foxnews.com/opinion/parents-furious-over-schools-plan-to-teach-gender-spectrum-fluidity.

49. Fraga, B. (2018). Does California law deny parents' right to opt out of "gender education"? *National Catholic Register* (9 May).

50. Adely, H. (2019). Can parents opt out of New Jersey's LGBTQ curriculum law? NorthJersey.com (6 June).

51. Brown, E., Chandler, M.A., and Balingit, M. (2015). Schools grapple with how to teach about Paris attacks. *The Washington Post* (16 November).

52. Bardolf, D. (2023). Pro-Israel parents booted from heated school board meeting. *The New York Post* (18 November). https://nypost.com/2023/11/18/metro/pro-israel-parents-booted-from-heated-school-board-meeting/.

53. Waxman, O.B. (2021). "Critical race theory is simply the latest bogeyman." Inside the fight over what kids learn about America's history. *TIME* (24 June). https://time.com/6075193/critical-race-theory-debate/.

54. Mizelle, S. and Wilson, K. (2023). House passes GOP education bill that aims to provide additional oversight for parents. CNN (24 March). https://www.cnn.com/2023/03/24/politics/house-vote-parents-bill-of-rights-act/index.html.

3

Why Parents Must Be Agents of Change

"Within a sociocultural framework, children's views are not finished products. Rather, they are formed and shaped in interaction with other people—children as well as adults."[1]

Parenting is hard. Prepared as we think we might be, raising children comes with all sorts of unknowns. Though hard, most parents strive to do their best to raise children to lead happy and healthy lives. In young childhood this parenting focuses on good habit formation, an ability to self-regulate one's emotions, develop independence and the ability for a child to care for themselves. As children get older, parents must show them how to navigate friendship and eventually relationships. They must teach them about school, homework, and extracurricular activities. Parents must develop strategies to talk about harder topics like drugs, alcohol, and sex. And to raise a child who can be a powerful, participating citizen, parents must be willing to talk about politics and government.

Your own parents may have either shunned politics as an impolite topic of conversation or expressed negative views about politicians and government. You yourself may shy away from politics as a topic because it seems too painful or frustrating, or because you feel politically adrift or hopeless. What's more, there is a widespread, cross-cutting tendency to socialize our children to think politics is "dirty" or "only for egomaniacs" or that the "system is rigged." When that is the leading message on politics, it's not surprising that the smaller details on how to participate are lost. In 2020, only about 25% of 18- to 24-year-olds reported having political discussions with their parents.[2]

When our kids are young, we are told to child-proof everything and make the world safer for our growing ones to be a part of. We edit our language and subjects in efforts to "let kids be kids" and not worry about things outside of their control. If we do this too much or for too long, we hinder their ability to think and develop their own methods for processing and coping with new information. As our children approach voting age, it's important to straightforwardly discuss our system of government and stress their potential for a role within that system. This is not about overwhelming them with the weight of the world, but rather inviting them into a conversation that will soon be theirs to lead. It's about transitioning from protecting to preparing.

Why is it up to you to do it? Because right now, no other institution is up to the task. Studies show that school civics only play a marginal role and the likelihood that students vote is more rooted in the ways they experience civics *in the home*.[3]

If you feel like most people that our politics are broken, then you owe it to yourself and your children to be a point of change. You are the best teachers and example setters for your children. You have them in their formative years, and they look up to you to show them how to become an adult. For the rest of this chapter, I'll describe to you a set of reasons why it's good that you do this, and why your children will be happier and more prepared for life if you do.

By the end of this chapter, no matter what your starting point, I hope you'll be convinced that not talking about politics at all with your children—or only talking about the negative parts of politics—is detrimental not just to their future political agency, but to the overall health of our politics. Besides, there are many benefits to talking about politics with our kids: it helps them make sense of their world and develop important skills that can help them in college or their careers. They likely want to talk about politics, and in committing to having these conversations, we open up another way for our kids to know us and for us to know them. After going through the upsides, I hope that you'll warm to the job of starting conversations at home.

Parents Shape the Way Children Dream: Firefighter, Police, or Politician?

When we ask children what they want to be when they grow up, they say things like a pro athlete, content creator, musician, firefighter, veterinarian, doctor, teacher, or chef.[4] Oftentimes these career wishes are inspired by the people they've been exposed to, whether in real life or in stories. There aren't many stories geared for kids that stress political processes, so it's on us to figure out how to weave these pathways in.

Toys, coloring books, dress-up clothes, and television shows are filled with police officers and other government "helpers," like firefighters, but it's rare that the politicians, bureaucrats, or activated community members take center stage.

The reality is, we need elected officials and appointed bureaucrats to do establishment and oversight work so that the people in public uniforms have the funding and structures to operate. All too often, the political or governing roles are demonized while more publicly "active" roles are celebrated, or at least given a pass when negative actions occur. We do not have to raise our children this way. We can encourage the work of law enforcement and emergency management while also recognizing the contributions of politicians. We should strive to teach children that all public occupations contribute to society in different ways. We can do that through the stories we tell.

Many times, our children hear the negative aspects of politics that tend to push adults away, which can lead to frustration and a disinterest in understanding how our government works. It's up to us to recognize and appreciate the positive contributions made by politicians and government—even if that takes the effort of looking for it. If you have well-maintained road systems or a functioning public transportation network, let your kids know that's the work of government. If you've got public schools that serve your community well, that's government at play. If you've got clean drinking water, that's government efforts. Did a new park open or get a renovation? Someone in local government had a hand in that effort. There are examples all around us, and it's up to us to point these bright spots out to kids.

These examples, though seemingly small, demonstrate the benefits that arise from government. By sharing these positive aspects of politics with our children, we can instill in them an appreciation for the role these institutions play in our daily lives. Appreciation doesn't have to mean free from all criticism. Things can, of course, always be better, but injecting some of the good parts can serve as a buffer for when government actions let us down.

A narrative exclusively focused on the negative aspects can discourage children from exploring and understanding the complexities of politics and government. When you see something in your community that is going well, try to figure out which agencies or elected officials had a hand in that, and be willing to share that praise with your kids.

Getting kids excited about being citizens is about instilling a sense of civic pride and emphasizing the importance of contributing to the betterment of society. By highlighting the roles and responsibilities of different professionals that make up pieces of the government, such as teachers, firefighters, politicians, community volunteers, and even bureaucrats, children can develop a more well-rounded understanding of the collective efforts that make our society function.

Children Are Inadvertently Curious About "Politics"

Childhood establishes and reinforces all the basic interpersonal systems we need to function as a society. We learn how to give, take, and, most importantly, share. We learn ownership and possessiveness—to assert "that's *my* toy!" in arguments with siblings or on the playground. We learn that sometimes "mine" is more fun when shared with others, like playing games with friends. We learn that there are some goods that are not strictly owned by any one person, such as a slide or a swing on a public playground. In shared spaces, children learn the value of negotiation, or parents enforce taking turns, providing a model for behavior.

Settings where different individuals have different goals (e.g., two children who want to play on a swing) are basic training grounds for compromise and equity, which also happen to be the cornerstone ideals of a democratic system. To establish who gets to play on the swing first, we might ask which child arrived at the swing first, who mentioned wanting to go to the park to swing, who generally enjoys that feature of the playground more, and what amount of time is fair to use a swing before giving it to another kid. Parents all over, regardless of circumstance, seize opportunities to give children these sorts of first-order lessons. Siblings and friends struggle over their own self-interest versus the interest of others when they fight for toys or argue over which game to play. Getting what you want and having to work with others is basic politics. In this realm, parents provide fairness frameworks for children, doing what they can to promote peace.

If you have ever heard a negotiation among children playing a game, you know how much they tend to care about rules and roles, which are centralizing pieces of governance. Imagine a group of children playing a game of make-believe in a park. They decide to create their own mini-society with rules and roles. As they engage in the game, they start negotiating and discussing various aspects, such as who gets to be the leader, how resources should be distributed, and how conflicts should be resolved. Each child expresses their opinions and in doing so advocates for their preferred rules and roles. In this scenario, you can see how much children care about the fairness, structure, and decision-making processes within their play society. As a parent, we can recognize and respect this sort of emerging political awareness.

Childhood should be fun. I am not suggesting that after little Benjamin and Xavier decide who gets the bigger slice of cake that their parents should launch into a lecture on budgeting negotiations in Congress. But it is my suggestion that when issues like budget breakdowns or government shutdowns capture national attention, parents should have the knowledge and wherewithal to talk to their children about these issues and be able to use examples from childhood day-to-day negotiations along the way.

Older Children Want to Know About Politics

A recent survey of teens aged 13–17 found that 78% of respondents said it was important to them to follow current events.[5] This same survey also found that teens attribute their current events knowledge to different sources: one-third said they used major news organizations in various mediums, one-third said they turned to influencers or celebrities, and one-third said they relied on their parents, others in their families, or teachers. Knowing this, parents who are hesitant to connect with their children over politics may find comfort in the apparent reality that many kids *want* to know more.

People who regularly work with children indicate that many kids don't like to feel left out or shielded from politics. There is a curiosity and interest even in the things that may seem too adult to many parents. Christine French Cully, the editor-in-chief of the children's education/entertainment empire *Highlights*, gave an interview in 2020 where she said that, "Kids are interested in talking about the election and politics. Researchers tell us this. And a lot of parents are reluctant to do so in a way that's meaningful, and that can help kids understand what it means to be a thoughtful, engaged citizen."

Her pulse on this issue squares with my understanding of the 18-year-olds I interact with in their first college classroom. They want to know things, and the allure of the "adult" world of politics exists. Not all children will want to have scheduled, serious government talk sessions, but most will be interested in having their questions considered. Maturity is something that most tweens and teens aspire to demonstrate to others, and practice talking about things in the political realm is one route to doing that.

By the time children enter their later teen years, they often have a strong desire to assert their independence and take charge of their own lives. We can all relate to that feeling of telling our own parents that they just didn't understand us. While teenagers may experience shifts in their interest and involvement in politics and activism, it is up to us to equip them with knowledge about how politics and government operate. Regardless of our preferences, politics will inevitably become a part of their lives. As they head to college or their first job, they will encounter new friends and be exposed to different political ideas. Our goal is not to *protect* them from politics or government (which is impossible), but rather to use the time we have with them before they leave home to *prepare* them for meaningful engagement in the political world.

One event of recent political history that some children of today will remember is the January 6, 2021, domestic attack on the U.S. Capitol. Some kids might recall that time as a fearful example of how politics can get violent, and that may induce anxiety or fear about being interested in politics. But that doesn't need to be the only framing parents can use for that event; rather, this can be an opportunity to talk about the challenges of politics as points of possibility to make a more harmonious political landscape.

January 6th can be discussed as an example of a concerning incident that highlights the importance of understanding politics and engaging in constructive dialogue. Parents can explain that such events are not representative of the entirety of politics but rather reflect a certain set of individuals' or groups' actions—and largely one that had a lower level of understanding of government procedures. It can be an opportunity to emphasize the need for respect, critical thinking, and peaceful methods of expressing dissent or seeking change.

Talking About Politics Allows Our Kids to Be Better Advocates and to Develop Important Life Skills

Children are better off when they can advocate for themselves, and politics is just a game of advocacy. Every day, in big ways and small, politics plays a role in shaping our lives. By providing our children with an understanding of political processes and encouraging their participation, we show them how to become active contributors to their communities, rather than just bystanders. And when children are equipped with the skills to advocate for themselves, to feel effective and capable of changing their lives, they are more likely to thrive academically, build stronger relationships, and be better positioned to succeed overall.

Effective advocacy stems from the development of a collection of "noncognitive" skills. As opposed to cognitive skills, which refer to the different processing functions that our brain uses to solve problems or store knowledge, noncognitive skills include other traits such as motivation, determination, and personal efficacy. These are things we want our children to have and must to work to cultivate. Research shows that traits like grit and determination have a greater impact on civic participation than mere fact retention or intelligence, so when you're talking politics with your kids, it shouldn't be focused on just getting the facts right. The process of being willing to have hard conversations repeatedly helps them hone important noncognitive skills.[6]

Practicing civic skills like research, listening, participation, and advocacy not only contributes to political development but is also related to the growth of empathy, emotion regulation, moral reasoning, and future-orientation.[7] By valuing these skills, and practicing with them, we equip our children with the tools they need to navigate the complexities of politics and in turn impact their own lives. When you take the lead, you provide a trusted and safe environment for your children to explore complex issues, ask questions, and express opinions, all of which help them develop their own positions and eventually work to advocate for those stances.

What's more, the National Conference on Citizenship has consistently reported that communities with greater rates of civic engagement have lower rates of unemployment.[8] Communities that collectively care about the future tend to be those that create systems that work for greater numbers of people. At the individual level, civic engagement and the associated gains in social capital and organizing skills can be parlayed into educational and economic opportunities.[9] The benefits are clear: caring about a community helps both individuals and our society.

Having a Better Understanding About Politics Contributes to Positive Mental Health

In addition to raising determined and self-advocating children, we all want healthy children. In many ways some of the major mental health issues that plague our children, such as anxiety, depression, and poor emotional regulation, find roots in a sense of hopelessness and helplessness. News headlines about politics on any given day are filled with these same feelings with added touches of outrage. We can turn things around. We may not be able to fix everything, but we can give our children different tools and strategies to deal with the sometimes-frustrating world of politics. We should let our children dream of a better politics, and not guide them into thinking it's all a rigged and losing game. It's not, but it is hard work and requires a little know-how and a lot of determination to show them a better way. By showing them how to think about hard issues and modeling a way for them to have hard conversations, parents give their children great life lessons that involve both skill and will. These components combine to create the amorphous concept of "character" that allows children to craft more fulfilling lives for themselves.

Having a better understanding of politics contributes to positive mental health in several ways. In the most basic sense, politics often involves issues that directly impact people's lives, such as healthcare, education, and the environment. When people have a deeper understanding of these issues and how they are influenced by political decisions, they can better assess who is working toward political goals that they agree or disagree with. Thinking that some abstract, faceless "government" is to blame isn't calming at all. In knowing some more of the process details, and the people who make up that government, people don't need to feel as afraid or overwhelmed by something that seems mysterious. Second, being politically engaged means having a voice to participate in shaping the policies and systems— that sort of efficacy is powerful. When people actively engage in political activities such as voting, advocacy, or community organizing, they experience a sense of purpose and meaning, which is a much better mental place to operate from.

Understanding politics makes it easier to navigate and to critically analyze information in the media and public discourse. By being able to discern the reliability of sources of information, evaluate different perspectives, and engage in informed discussions, people are less likely to feel confused, or manipulated. This ability to engage with political information is a way to reduce the stress and anxiety that fill the pages and screens of our news.

Lastly, politics is inherently social, involving interactions with others who hold different views and beliefs. Developing the skills to engage in respectful and constructive political discourse can reduce the potential for conflict or isolation. In involving your kids in the social aspect of politics, they'll be able to widen their own networks and be able to practice discussions with different people. Showing them the way to find politically active people and groups means that their likelihood for isolation later in life will be reduced.

Talking About Politics Helps Kids Get into College

When it comes to college admissions, test scores and GPAs are important factors, but there is also a growing emphasis on a student's potential to contribute to society. Colleges and universities want students who will succeed in life, not just for potential benefits of alumni donations, but also as examples to recruit future students and build their own reputation. When it comes time to apply for college, having a résumé or essay that can speak to how a student has navigated a political system or engaged with government in the past is a strong way to signal that they care about bigger societal issues.

A child who engages with civics on their own terms demonstrates initiative and know-how. Even when not successful, the gumption and willingness to work toward a goal is an attractive quality. As your child matures, if they express an interest in getting to know a government official, you may have to pave the way for the initial introductions, but then get out the way and allow your child to speak up for themselves and their position. Let them ask about interning or doing volunteer work for an office or politician.

Even if your child doesn't become a government whiz kid, in her book *The Smartest Kids in the World: And How They Got*

That Way, Amanda Ripley describes that the children who report having more frequent dinner time conversations with their parents about things like current events tend to score better on the Programme for International Student Assessment test. When discussing civics with your kids, you aren't teaching to the test; you are teaching the value of a critical thinking process and showing them how to reason and work through issues. These lessons amplify anything else learned in formal schooling. This is just another way that these sorts of discussions can prepare your child for college and the entrance exams that come along with that process.

Talking About Politics with Your Kids Is Good for You Too

Talking through politics with our children helps us reflect on our own political thoughts and allows us to engage with their youthful perspective. Children, with their open and less prejudicial approach to things, provide us with an opportunity to question and examine our own knowledge and political preferences. Children pose both simple *and* challenging questions that can prompt introspection. I know my daughter has asked loads of questions that leave me thinking about things long after our conversation is over.

A simple example that any child learning about politics will eventually ask of a parent is, "Are you a Democrat or a Republican?" Parents who have a clear political identification may find this easy to answer. For those of us still figuring things out, that's much harder. But for everyone, the inevitable follow-up question of "why" is more complex. These sorts of questions from our kids offer us adults a chance to work through our own reasoning. By embracing political conversations with your kids, you'll also be providing a valuable way to work on your own for personal growth and self-reflection.

Talking about politics with children allows us to refine our own vision of politics. We all have different lived experiences, and by having these discussions as a family, we can show children *and* adults how different people approach and think about issues. We can start to think about which sorts of issues or areas we'd like to learn more about or be active in. We can think about what sorts of characteristics we want in our elected leaders. We can talk about what issues our kids care about, and what they can do on those as they find their own sorts of political power.

By engaging in political conversations at home, parents can create a ripple effect, encouraging discussions among their childrens' peers and even with their peers' own parents. These conversations become a valuable addition to the other topics we as parents seek advice on, such as puberty, relationships, and schooling. Increasing the space for political dialogue in your home is a small, but consequential part in creating a society where we can address issues, understand different aspects of government, and reduce mistrust. Such intergenerational discussions are critical for the survival and growth of democracy, older people have things to teach and learn, and younger people need to see us model this sort of behavior. The functioning of our government relies on the collective understanding and informed choices of its citizens. With an accurate understanding of how our government works, we can strive for a more functional political system.

No One Knows Everything

A lot of parenting guides tell parents to act as authority figures—according to them, children behave when they understand their parents are the boss. But no one knows everything, so if we're supposed to be the boss all the time, sometimes that means stretching our own understanding of an issue, or even resorting to "because I said so." When talking about government or policy issues that you are unsure of, be comfortable with saying, "I don't know," and following up with your own questions with your child. You can create a set of things to figure out together and then go about doing just that. We live in a time of incredible tools—many of which are readily at hand in our phones—to at least start the process of figuring things out together. When you don't know something, know that you can probably figure it out with enough time using the resources you already have; doing that alongside your child will be fun and will let you both learn about how each other searches for answers.

Let's say you have an election happening in your town. Suppose your child asks why certain people should be elected and others should not—maybe they heard about a certain candidate at school or online. In this example, you might not know all the details about each candidate, but you can discuss the principles of democracy, such as the right to vote, the idea that anyone can run for office, and the importance of a fair election process. Better yet, you can agree to sit down together for 20 minutes or so and learn what you can about different candidates together. Using your phones or computers, you and your child can visit candidate websites, watch videos, and read articles discussing that specific office and the candidates. Together, you and your child can discuss the information you find, think about why you might be fed different results through algorithmic searches than what they will find, ask follow-up questions of one another, and analyze different sources to develop a well-rounded understanding about the people and the election that you've decided to look into.

Throughout this research journey, parents should emphasize the importance of questioning, critical thinking, and utilizing different sorts of tools to find accurate information. No one media type or source will have all the answers. Like researching any sort of topic, it takes many different input to really start to understand something. In my experience both parents and kids alike will enjoy the process of discovery—as long as both are committed to doing it. By exploring a new topic together, parents and kids not only find answers but also strengthen their bonds as both sides work through their thought process and go back and forth in assessing a candidate.

In this example, a parent who doesn't know the specifics of a local election demonstrates the willingness to acknowledge their own limitations while encouraging curiosity and active engagement with their child. A parent who does that is modeling good civic-minded behavior for their child. They show the importance of continuous learning and resourcefulness, with a sense of intellectual curiosity in a way that shows kids it's worth learning more.

Your children don't need you to know everything. They need you to show them that it's possible to learn more. They need you to show them that no one knows everything and that we all have room to grow. Besides, if you give an answer that's wrong—just to feel like you gave an answer—your child will someday learn the more correct answer and have reason to mistrust what you say about these things. Modeling what happens when you don't know something is a valuable thing to impart to your children, and we've all got blind spots when it comes to politics.

Not Raising Clones

There is no way to ensure that your kids will see politics in the same way you do, and that's for the best. Our system relies on change and a variety of different approaches and viewpoints to evolve. Yet for some very invested parents, it might come as a blow if you raise a child who turns out to be closer to what you consider political opposition than ally. Do not fret too much on this. It is not even clear that you could indoctrinate your children to see the world as you do if you wanted to. But that should not be your aim, and if it is, it might even backfire.[10] The goal of this work is for us to learn about each other and how we can work together.

This book speaks very infrequently about the issue of partisanship. Teaching you how to raise little Democrats or little Republicans is not the purpose. Besides, anyone who tells you that they can show you how to do that is not being honest. The research on raising children who see the political world in exactly the way we do is mixed at best. Some studies find that children growing up in homes where politics are never or rarely talked about tend to have political preferences that are more similar to their parents, but these homes also tend to be some of the least politically engaged.[11] Other research rooted in social learning theory finds that parents' political orientations can be directly transmitted to children if the family is highly politicized and if parents provide consistent cues over time.[12] But still other research questions the ability of parents to transmit political partisanship to children without considering how children's use and trust of media disrupts familial partisan socialization.[13]

The bottom line is that raising a citizen is different than raising a partisan. For the goal of making a better-functioning body politic, creating a set of more robustly interested and informed citizens is better than having a set of pledged partisans.

We can teach our children the basics and accept that they may come to different conclusions than we do. If fissures emerge on the path of discussing politics and government with your children between your views and theirs, it is not your job to seal them up. By doing the work of having these sometimes-hard conversations early on with your children, you will teach them to appreciate others even when they have differences of opinion. That skill should serve them well into adulthood.

Conclusion

A population that is unwilling or unable to talk about politics and government makes political and societal problems harder to solve. Ignorance makes the machinery of politics less open and harder to engage with because not enough people have a working knowledge of how things are set up. A lack of knowledge leaves us feeling ineffective, a lack of interest leaves us feeling out of control, and a lack of understanding provides a breeding ground for mistrust and even political violence.

Whatever the rationale, the notion that not talking about politics "solves" anything is incorrect. Politics and government are inevitable, so different parts will get to our kids in one way or another. Additionally, research spanning decades consistently highlights the importance of multiple sources of information when it comes to understanding how to vote and cultivating a habit of civic participation.[14] You might as well be the first point of contact for such a consequential topic.

We are raising kids to be adults. And part of being an adult ought to be considering oneself a citizen capable of facing the political problems of the day. It is not as if a magic element of voting and government knowledge somehow appears when someone turns 18. It is up to us as parents to play a role in making sure these lessons are a part of childhood, but also allow space for kids to figure things out on their own. In the next chapter, I describe how you can start the work of talking about politics and government in your home.

Notes

1. Ulvik, O.S. (2015). Talking with children: Professional conversations in a participation perspective. *Qualitative Social Work 14* (2): 193–208.
2. Amandi, F., Williams, A., Feldman, D., et al. (2020). The 100 million project. The untold story of American non-voters. The Knight Foundation.
3. Weinschenk, A.C. and Dawes, C.T. (2020). Civic education in high school and voter turnout in adulthood. *British Journal of Political Science*: 1–15.
4. In a survey study of the top 20 things children said they wanted to be when they grow up, politician at any level did not make the list. Kocher, S. (2001). These are the most popular jobs kids dream of doing when they grow up. SWNS Digital (6 September) https://swnsdigital .com/us/2019/12/these-are-the-most-popular-jobs-kids-dream-of-doing-when-they-grow-up/. Bruce, G. (2021). Doctor, vet, esports star, influencer: Dream jobs among US teens. YouGov (14 December). https://today.yougov.com/technology/articles/39997-influencer-dream-jobs-among-us-teens.
5. Common Sense Media. (2019). Teen News Engagement: Key Findings and Toplines. https://www.commonsensemedia.org/sites/default/files/research/report/2019_cs-sm_summarytoplines_release.pdf.
6. Holbein, J.B. and Hillygus, D.S. (2020). *Making Young Voters: Converting Civic Attitudes into Civic Action*. New York: Cambridge University Press.
7. Metzger, A., Alvis, L.M., Oosterhoff, B., et al. (2018). The intersection of emotional and sociocognitive competencies with civic engagement in middle childhood and adolescence. *Journal of Youth and Adolescence 47* (8): 1663–1683.
8. The National Conference on Citizenship (NCoC) is a nonpartisan, nonprofit organization dedicated to strengthening civic life in America.
9. Benenson, J. (2017). Civic engagement and economic opportunity among low-income individuals: An asset-based approach. *VOLUNTAS: International Journal of Voluntary and Nonprofit Organizations* 28 (3): 988–1014.
10. Areu, C. (2016). I just wanted my kids to share my politics; turns out, I was doing it wrong. Today (27 September). https://www.today.com/parents/i-just-wanted-my-kids-share-my-politics-turns-out-t103343.

11. De Landtsheer, C., Kalkhoven, L., Heirman, W., and De Vries, P. (2018). Talking politics at the dinner table: Stereotypes in children's political choices. *PCS–Politics, Culture and Socialization* 7 (1+2): 19–20.
12. Jennings, M.K, Stoker, L., and Bowers. J. (2009). Politics across generations: Family transmission reexamined. *The Journal of Politics 71* (3): 782–799.
13. Buckingham, D. (1999). Young people, politics and news media: Beyond political socialisation. *Oxford Review of Education 25* (1–2): 171–184.
14. Wray-Lake, L. (2019). How do young people become politically engaged? *Child Development Perspectives 13* (2): 127–132.

CHAPTER

4

How to Have Political Conversations

In 2022, the Supreme Court's decision in *Dobbs v. Jackson Women's Health Organization* overturned the 1973 decision *Roe v. Wade*, which recognized a woman's right to an abortion up to 24 weeks. This ruling ignited passions among parents of all political stripes and inevitably made its way into the ears of children and teens. My 10-year-old, new to the topic, asked, "What is an abortion?"

I was raised in a home where this sort of question might be dismissed or covered with, "I'll tell you about it to you when you're older."

Choosing transparency over vagueness, I explained pregnancy—which she had a decent grasp on already—and described abortion as a medical procedure that interrupts this process. We discussed the spectrum of beliefs about when, if at all, abortion is acceptable, touching on the nuances of life, viability, and differing state laws. I knew if I didn't give her an answer, a query to "Alexa" or a search on a computer would put all sorts of information and imagery in front of her. I thought about what language and conceptual imagery would give my daughter the tools to think about this issue in a way relevant for her age while still doing justice to the broader debate. She asked a lot of questions during this conversation.

Using the lens of our home state, New York, I contrasted our laws with those of Mississippi to illustrate the varying political climates. When we talked about why the Supreme Court had reason at all to weigh in on the subject, I described the role of courts as "referees" in settling disputes, much like a parent mediates children's disagreements.

In the course of this talk, we got into the concept of *federalism*, stressing that while nothing would likely change immediately in our state, in others, access to abortion would, and that political action could further influence these laws. Throughout our talk, I maintained a neutral tone, which can be difficult to manage on such a large and challenging topic. I encouraged her curiosity, and followed her lead, ensuring the discussion remained informative yet age appropriate.

You can do the same in your home.

In the precious time we have with our children in our homes, we've got to discuss collective decision-making, government systems, and civic engagement. It's an ongoing journey, and a beautiful way to teach and learn from our kids. These talks, while sometimes complex, are necessary for their development. By initiating or at least being receptive and responsive to these conversations, you can become a resource to your kids in a whole new way *and* demonstrate the importance of understanding politics.

Whether you're a political insider or just starting to learn about the political world, it's important to talk to your children about these topics. If you have extensive knowledge about politics, embrace the opportunity to share your passion and expertise, all with the aim to letting them develop their own sorts of interests in the subject. Help your children understand different perspectives by being willing to research positions outside of your own. If you have reservations or lack familiarity with political topics, don't let that deter you from exploring these conversations. Show your kids that it's worthwhile to learn about things you don't know, especially those that can affect your life as much as politics can. By expanding your own understanding of government and politics by reading through the second half of this book, you can start to provide insights to your children and be better prepared to navigate any additional topics you want to learn about together.

We sometimes hear calls for a "national conversation" for policies ranging from prescription drug access to gun ownership and everything in between. A national conversation is not one thing that happens; it's a set of smaller conversations all over the nation, at home with our families and friends, with a willingness to listen and to understand. By doing this in having these sorts of discussions with your children, you make them more capable to address political challenges that arise when they become the adults in charge of our system.

You know your children best. Tune into their interests and readiness when choosing topics and timing for these conversations. Be open to their questions, and rather than deferring the discussion for when they're older, provide age-appropriate explanations now. Their reactions, whether inquisitive or indifferent, are all fine. What matters is that you've welcomed the dialogue and shown that political discourse is a part of life they can be involved in.

There are three things to keep in mind when talking about politics and government with your kids at any age: recognizing your role, restraining your own negativity, and being willing to research and reach out.

First, you must recognize your pivotal role in shaping your children's understanding and perspectives on politics and government. You are the person they get to spend the most time around and the person they most look up to when thinking about how to become an adult. Because of this, you are the primary model they will look to for guidance on how to interpret and engage with the world around them—politics included. In recognizing your role, this means you need to show them how you learn about and discuss political issues. Like with everything else about parenting, the way to approach things will be the way your kids first come to understand something, so be mindful of that. Show them that you are open to these sorts of conversations so they know they can come to you. This means providing them with different perspectives, acknowledging the complexity of political issues, and letting them know that your home is an environment where questioning and respectful debate are encouraged.

In building from this recognition, the second thing you need to be willing to do is restrain your own negativity. Though this might not come easily, it's one that I cannot stress enough. If our kids grow up hearing us only disparaging politics and government figures, they are far less likely to want to learn more, do more, or engage in politics in a way that is productive. It's certainly okay to have strong opinions about political issues and figures— and you want to be someone that your kids can come to if they have strong opinions—but showing restraint in how *you* express these sentiments is incredibly important. Using insults or slurs to describe politicians—even those you disagree with—does not make for better or more functional politics. As you know, children are highly perceptive and will easily pick up on your outlook, which can color their own views before they have a chance to fully understand the issues at hand. Instead, try to show them the value of open-mindedness and how to disagree with people or ideas without resorting to name-calling. If all they experience is negativity, they will likely either disengage from politics or also come into things with a negative view, not open to a learning mindset.

Third—and perhaps the part that requires the most effort from you—is to research and reach out to an elected official to humanize government. You don't have to fly to DC to make this happen—though that is a neat thing to experience. You just need to be willing to research and reach out to local or state elected officials and seek opportunities for you and your child to meet with them. If a one-on-one meeting seems too daunting, go to a member's office and meet their staff and learn about something happening in your area. All politicians are just people, and state and local politicians are likely to be running around to events close to your home. Do a little background research and try to be at one of these events and say hello. Humanizing government by introducing your kids to the people who serve in those roles shows them a tangible and understandable form of government, versus the amorphous behemoth that most of us conjure up in our minds. These interactions work to demystify the political process, and show your children that politicians are accessible and that their work has direct implications on everyday life. If your child gets along with or looks up to a certain politician, that might be a good connection to work from as they get older and think about summer internships or jobs. If they don't like the politician, that might serve as fuel to think about different forms of leadership. And if they don't much care either way—as will happen with a number of kids—that's still great because they have now put a human to an idea and will better be able to understand the sorts of people who make up government.

Talking About Politics and Government with Kids of Different Ages

There is no one-size-fits-all approach to discussing complex subjects like politics—everything has a context, and every person has a unique way of processing information. The aim in talking to our kids about politics isn't to turn them into government trivia experts but simply to show that these discussions are good to have.

Early on, when your kids are young, you're just setting up a mental framework for your child, rather than getting into details. As children grow, their abilities to grasp certain concepts change—what seems irrelevant to a young child becomes clearer for an older one nearing voting age. You know this, because everything about parenting is constantly changing, and kids can handle more and more of our reality as they get older. Tailor conversations to your child's developmental stage, laying the groundwork in the earlier years, and building to more concrete examples as they become teens. Younger children, especially in elementary school, often focus on the present moment. When discussing politics, remember their perspective, keeping talks relevant to their immediate world—giving them a set of hypotheticals to ponder just doesn't work as well at that age, but giving them examples that they can relate to does.

For instance, when talking to a five-year-old about leadership as a quality in people, you might compare it to how a teacher manages a classroom, setting rules and helping students, or how a coach manages a team or a director manages a cast, picking certain things to focus on in practice or rehearsal and how to motivate good performances at game or show time. As that child becomes a teenager, you could discuss leadership in terms of a mayor or president, exploring how they make decisions that affect a city or country. When talking about leadership, you can ask your kids to think about the leaders they have liked in all different sorts of contexts and ask them to find any similarities to the politicians who represent you.

I've broken ages into three categories: young grade school kids (5–9), pre-adolescent and young adolescents (10–14), and more independent teenagers (15–18). By understanding the appropriate concepts and approaches for each age group, you can start conversations in ways that make sense across different ages. For teenagers, I provide detailed questions and strategies you can use to explore their political interests more deeply.

The key to discussing politics with children is simply to begin. If you are unsure about a topic, show your kids that you're open to their questions and eager to learn together. What counts is the quality of your interaction, not how much you cover. Engaging in these exchanges is what matters most, not necessarily what's talked about. This is because by showing them how to have these conversations they will be better able to enter similar conversations with their peers or other mentors, so if you don't cover everything yourself, that's perfectly fine. They will have a mental model of how these conversations work, and that's a great head start for contemplating things about politics and government.

Young Childhood, 5–9 Years Old

Kids who are in early grade school care much more about *people* than concepts or processes.[1] When my daughter was younger, she was able to recognize local officials she'd met but found the electoral college concept elusive (if it's still blurry for you too, don't worry, I'll break it down in Chapter 6). When talking civics with young kids, focus on the individuals in government roles, providing visuals and relatable stories when possible.

In years past, it was much harder to find an elected official that looked different than a standard, middle-to-older-age white man. And though there is still work to do in representation, today there are examples of politicians from many more backgrounds and identities. When exposing your kids to politicians through pictures, show them some that "look like" them or share some traits with your own child so that they too may have an empowering visual model. Children may also be interested in meeting local politicians like your city council member or mayor, and those offices are usually happy to oblige these sorts of requests.

Election seasons are filled with ads and news stories that make for easy opportunities to discuss the role of the president and members of Congress as well as the voting process. Involve children in simple family votes to demystify the concept. Kids at this age can grasp broad concepts like fairness and patriotism, and as they see political ads, you can discuss campaign promises that you hear together. And of course, children at any age are suitable companions for the voting booth. Taking them to see the machines and process can be interesting to them, and they'll be sure to charm all the election officials by just coming in with you. On the way to making young voters, you really should take your kids to vote with you. Though the timing can be hard, and in some instances waits can be long, it's important that they have a tradition of voting and understand the experience of what it takes to vote. By bringing them with you to the polls, you familiarize them with the experience of the process in ways that descriptions simply can't capture.

There are a set of books geared to this age that do a nice job of working through harder political concepts with relatable stories and characters. Two of my favorites are *One Vote, Two Votes, I Vote, You Vote* by Bonnie Worth and Aristides Ruiz as well as *Duck for President* by Doreen Cronin and Betsy Lewin. I've even had my college students read *One Vote, Two Votes, I Vote, You Vote* out loud as a class and stopped at any point where the book mentions something that everyone in the class does not already understand. Every year we have multiple stopping points.

Brad Meltzer's *I am* book series is another good choice for introducing little kids to politicians and historical figures.

Meltzer has a way of making historical figures accessible to young readers. He presents facts about his subject and their achievements in a narrative format, in a way that can make politicians interesting for even the youngest learners. His series includes stories about George Washington, Abraham Lincoln, Ruth Bader Ginsburg, John Lewis, Harriet Tubman, and more.

While young children are mostly outside formal politics, they're not irrelevant. If you have a child who really wants to get involved and do more at a young age, they can engage in politics by writing or drawing to legislators, creating postcard pictures for upcoming elections, initiating community projects, and participating in local activism. Encourage these activities and support their interests. You'll have to help them send their work to elected officials, but in partnering with them, you show that you value their civic mindedness in a way that should stay with them as they get older. You want to be the parent whose kid looks back and says, "Mom really did support me!"

Adolescents, 10–14 Years Old

As kids mature into later grade school and middle school ages, they perceive politics as more than just personalities; they see it as part of the larger systems that shape society. Their scope of appreciation is still limited, but they can handle more complex topics, such as historical political debates, and current events. Schools often start those sorts of conversations, even if they don't seem overtly political. One strategy is to discuss topics that align with their school curriculum and try to bridge parts of history that they might be learning about with things happening today. As a parent, you have much more leeway with what you can talk about with your kids than schoolteachers do.

Let's say your child is learning about the American Revolution in school, specifically about the Boston Tea Party and the idea of "no taxation without representation." This historical event can be a springboard for a discussion on the general role of protests in democracy. You could ask why the colonists protested, and after listening to their answer you likely will be able to make a connection to another sort of reason protests happen today. Exploring the similarities and differences over time will be a way to show the power of people in politics.

As kids of this age gain independence and start to understand group dynamics, it's a perfect time for discussions about collective decision-making and the value of voting. They're ready to consider broader ideas, like party platforms, and can engage in meaningful activities that reflect their burgeoning values, like school clubs or community service. They might even have elections of their own for school government to participate in.

Though these children will eventually outgrow picture books, engaging physical books are still a way to catch their attention. For a hard copy resource, *The Interactive Constitution* by David Miles has a set of fold-out and spin-style page tricks to draw attention to key concepts in government. The Big Ideas Series includes *The Politics Book: Big Ideas Simply Explained*. It doesn't get into details but does offer a way to have many different sorts of conversations about larger topics.

Videos, like political ads, offer real-time learning opportunities, and engaging with elected officials becomes more tangible. Children this age can advocate for local changes, like improved community sports facilities, and learn how to interact with government officials firsthand.

Children ages 10–14 are more capable than younger children in writing, creating art, or making interactive media that can be shared with those in government. If you find that your child has an issue that he or she would like to raise with an elected official, encourage and help them to contact the member with their idea. By preparing some sort of document, memo, graphic, drawing, meme, or set of video clips, your child has a better chance of standing out to an elected official and increases the likelihood that they'll be able to forge a direct connection. These sorts of attempts allow kids to see politicians as responsive people in our system.

There are also occasionally local or federal contests designed to get kids involved in politics such as the annual Congressional App Challenge and the annual Congressional Art Competition. In 2022, Ulster County New York held a design contest to see who could create the best "I Voted" sticker to be given to voters on Election Day. I was delighted when a 14-year-old won the contest with a highly nontraditional sticker design (see Figure 4.1).

FIGURE 4.1 The 2022 winning "I Voted" sticker for Ulster County, designed by Hudson Rowan.

Children at this developmental stage often form opinions on things that affect their lives, which tend to be local or state issues like school lunch quality or the condition of sports fields. For instance, if your child is disappointed by the missing rims at local basketball courts, this could be an opportunity to engage with local government. Here's how you can do that:

- Talk with your child about the missing rims at the basketball court and explain that such community issues are managed by local authorities.

- Together, explore your local government's website to identify the officials or committees responsible for parks and recreation.

- Find the specific official in charge of park facilities and plan how to contact them, starting with an email to voice your concerns. Help your child draft a polite email to the official, detailing the issue with the basketball court and requesting the installation of rims.

- It's also a good idea to reach out to the most local representative you have, which may be a city or town council person.

- If there's no reply within a week, teach your child how to follow up with a phone call to the official's office, guiding them through the process.

- If necessary, go to the local office with your child and set up an appointment to talk with your representative or someone from their constituent concerns staff. Being persistent pays off in politics.

Local officials generally *love* the opportunity to talk about how they hear from the community, and if your child has a good idea or one that a local politician or governmental official can work toward, that might be the start of an interesting back and forth for your kid. If you don't have success reaching out to and connecting with your local political actors, then you know there is some work to do. It can be very hard (though certainly not impossible) to get the attention and time of a federal politician, but for local or state issues, your elected officials should be willing to engage with you.

Usually, local officials enjoy engaging with the people they represent. It's why they sought their position in the first place. If your child proposes a viable idea, it might be possible to implement it, and that sort of work is something noticed by those higher up in government. For instance, in 2022, U.S. senator Joe Manchin recognized a student for leading a skatepark project, demonstrating how youth involvement can influence community improvements and receive acknowledgment.[2]

Teens and Young Adults, 15–18

For teens, the same advice for contacting officials applies as with younger kids, but they can also volunteer or work in political roles, oftentimes offering fresh perspectives on campaigns that older campaign staff members are keen to learn about. They can engage in activities like canvassing, running petitions for local issues, or participating in voter registration drives, even if they can't vote yet. Most states even allow teens to work as poll workers with excused absences from school, providing them with a firsthand experience of our fundamental political process.[3] Asking your child to do this once, and offering to do it with them, can be one of the best firsthand educational experiences of how voting works and I recommend it for everyone.

If working, interning, or volunteering is not something your teen wants to do, there are other resources that they'll probably like. Instead of reading, an audiobook like *The Everything*

American Government Book: From the Constitution to Present-Day Elections, All You Need to Understand Our Democratic System by Nick Ragone can be a way to introduce teens to political and government concepts without feeling like you're asking them to do additional reading on top of the increasing homework burden of these years. They could play it while exercising or driving to and from work. If you are lucky enough to have a child who still wants to have deep conversations with you at this age, offer to listen yourself and be willing to talk through parts that you've both finished.

Teens are old enough to grasp concepts like checks and balances, federalism, and fair voting. While they may initially dismiss news headlines or stories related to political institutions as uninteresting or boring, they are quite capable of engaging with these topics if they're willing. Many teens harbor cynicism or smugness toward authority and government—and some for very good reason[4]—but it's important to acknowledge and explore these perspectives rather than dismissing them as mere products of their age.

On the other hand, some teens are incredibly active in political movements like March for Our Lives and climate protests, often surpassing adults in their political activism. Each teenager is unique, and as a parent, you know your children best and can determine what to discuss and when. But nothing should be off limits at this stage; this is the final bit of preparation time we have before they head out into the world.

As our kids reach the age of leaving home, political discussions become more important and our window for influencing them narrows. Beyond conversation, one of the best things you can do for your child is show them how to register to vote. In a growing number of states, kids can pre-register to vote at age 16 or 17, becoming eligible to exercise the right to vote at age 18. Some states also permit 17-year-olds to vote in primary elections if they will turn 18 before the general election. Some local elections may permit 16- and 17-year-olds to participate, but all state and federal elections require that voters be 18.

In the following sections, I'll go over how to have these sorts of conversations with your child, but if you have 15- to 18-year-olds there are five things about voting that they must know in order to be able to fully participate in politics once they turn 18 and/or leave your home. I come back to this topic later, but while we are talking about teenagers, it bears highlighting this necessary information now. Here's what your teens need to understand to be able to start formally participating:

Voter Registration: Offer to do their first registration with them, emphasize its importance.

Address Changes: Explain that registration is linked to their physical address and must be updated with each move. With each move they have for the next few years, you can include a voter registration form or reminder in any care package you send. I still do this for friends well into adulthood.

Election Schedules: Teach them to find their local election calendar and inform them about early voting options where applicable.

Ballot Access: Clarify the differences in mail-in ballot rules— and let them know that different states have different systems to navigate.

Primary Types: Help them understand open versus closed primaries and how that affects their voting power.

Across All Ages

Introducing politics to kids is like wanting your children to develop an appreciation for music or art—it's about exposure.

Not every concept in math resonates with every student, but exposure opens doors to future passions and problem-solving abilities. This is why every school in the United States exposes children to math for multiple years. Similarly, by discussing a variety of political and governmental topics, you provide your children with opportunities to find their own interests over the years that you have with them.

As you guide your teen through political conversations, remember that it's about giving them an opportunity to learn, to try new things and ideas, to attempt to understand different viewpoints from different perspectives, and to find their own interests. Some may gravitate toward the strategy behind political campaigns, while others might be intrigued by the intricacies of law making, still others will want to know more about the impact of community organizing. Wherever their interests lie, be willing to follow up and learn more together.

Now for the fun part! In the upcoming sections, you'll find specific strategies to engage your children on political and governmental topics. You know your teen best, so while these tips can guide you, they're just starting points. You'll have to modify these conversations to fit your child's interests, and remember, the goal is to ignite curiosity, not to prescribe a certain political path.

How to Talk About Politics and Government

Remember, talking with your kids about politics doesn't require you to be an expert, it just requires that you be game to do it. Effective discussions are built on trust and a willingness to explore ideas together, not necessarily on the expertise of the participants. Researchers have found that when children initiate a conversation, families that have a good baseline of trust and connection are what's needed for functional political discussions at home.[5] So it's really not necessary for you to *know* everything; you have to be willing to talk things out and learn together. You can encourage openness in discussion with an invitation like:

> *"Hey, I'm open to discussing any concerns or questions you have about politics. Don't worry about getting things 'right'; we'll learn together. There's plenty I didn't know at your age, and there is plenty more for me to learn."*

Don't expect every chat to be lengthy or conclusive—this "conversation" can be made of lots of little discussions you have over their childhood. They may spring from a question during a car ride or come up during dinner or emerge as world events unfold. You are not going to get to a specific answer most of the time you talk about issues, but each time that you do you are showing them that it matters to think and talk about political matters.

Active listening is a key skill to use in discussions with your kids. These are not talks that you should do while distracted on your phone. Sure, you might be folding laundry together when you decide to talk about something but try to keep the more mental distractions separate from talk time. By being present in these conversations, you allow your children to articulate their thoughts with an active audience, and in turn they'll be more likely to be better listeners when you try to talk to them about any number of topics.

Try to hold on to the idea that your children are not necessarily challenging your views when they disagree with you, they're simply expressing their own. And it's okay for two different people to view things in different ways—that's really what a lot of politics is all about. Remain composed and welcome their perspective, even if it's unconventional or counter to those of your own. This privilege of exploration you provide is invaluable. Your kids will feel safe and therefore be better able to hold on to the conversations as they mature.

Ensure openness to their sources, thoughts, and questions about political subjects. They just got into this world, so it's not surprising if they come at issues in ways that are different than how you do. If any of discussions intensify, be sure to maintain your composure. Children's ideas, even extreme ones, are better moderated through dialogue with trusted adults. Media often depicts political talk as combative; your conversations need not follow that script. In particularly contentious or polarized topics, avoid partisan labels. Focus on the essence of the debate and why opinions vary. When sharing your stance, guide your teen through your reasoning, considering their input along the way. You likely will not set the *topic* since kids tend to ask about political issues more than the other way around, but you can set the *tone*.

Questions to Ask

I use a set of four questions when I have in-class discussions that easily can be used for talks inside the home. When a child shows interest in politics or government, the key is to engage thoughtfully. Don't rush to provide answers; instead, be willing to go further into their curiosity with these four guiding questions:

1. What have you *heard* about this issue?—This is my favorite question because it removes responsibility from the respondent to state an opinion or offer and idea that is their own. It's the easiest and best way to get a conversation going. It uncovers their information sources, laying the groundwork for their current understanding.

2. What do you *think* about this issue?—Focus on their perspective without pressing for justification. This is about acknowledging their views as they are.

3. What do you *know* about this issue?—This question separates knowledge from opinion, teaching them to value information alongside their feelings.

4. What *more do you want to know* about this issue?—This encourages them to think deeply and seek further information, a key element of critical thinking skills.

By starting with "What have you heard?" you open the doors as wide as can be and relieve a child from thinking they'll have to own or defend whatever they say. Maybe they *heard* something from another adult that they couldn't quite make sense of, but they've been thinking about it. Maybe they *heard* something through social media that seems really compelling, even if it's simple. But whatever the case, starting with a question that allows a child to simply go through all the inputs they've had on an issue is a way for them to express ideas that are both comforting and uncomfortable. And conversations are better with more information on the table to start with.

These questions help track a child's information sources, thoughts, existing knowledge, and learning desire. Notice that I leave out the question of "why." In guiding teens through political discussions, focus on *exploration* rather than interrogation. Avoid asking the follow-up "why" as it can prematurely pressure them to justify their thoughts. Instead, encourage them to share what they've heard, think, and know about an issue. Besides, they'll probably get to the "why" stage with you first, and then after you consider your answers, you can then turn that question back to them. This approach values their perspective and creates an environment of mutual learning. If there is a part you are confused about, ask if you can research something together. This doesn't have to be a term paper length project; it can be a pause to head online together to do some basic querying.

In talking politics with your kids, capitalize on their natural curiosity. Learning with your child not only builds their understanding but also strengthens your bond. It's of course important to clarify the distinction between personal views and factual knowledge. This clarity supports effective learning, turning curiosity into insight over time.

Encourage your child to articulate what they want to know more about. This can be reframed as "What do you need to learn to feel confident in your opinion?" or "What information might challenge your current view?" For older children, prompt them to examine different viewpoints. Encouraging this skill early on, under your guidance, helps your child mature into a thoughtful adult.

Let's pause here and use an example to show how these questions can work in action:

Teenage son: Being a police officer seems so dangerous. I'm not interested in work like that.

Parent: Oh, that's interesting. What have you heard that makes you think it's so dangerous?

Son: My friend, Ben, wants to become a cop, but I've heard it's like one of the deadliest jobs out there. It's hard for me to picture doing something that risky.

Parent: Hmm. What else do you think about that?

Son: I *think* he's not even considering other things he could do! He says he wants to stay in town and serve the community but policing just seems like the most dangerous choice. At our school's job fair, there were loads of safer community roles he could explore.

Parent: It's great you're both considering future careers. What do you two *know* about the on-the-job deaths for police officers versus other city jobs?

Son:	All I know is cops are always getting shot at, and I don't want anything to happen to Ben.
Parent:	Hmm . . . you *know* that? I'm not too sure about the risks myself, learning more sounds like a good thing to do. Want to team up and research this? What should we look for?
Son:	Maybe we could look up statistics on job-related fatalities. . . . I haven't heard of any deaths in other government jobs, though.
Parent:	Well, it's clear you care a lot about Ben's choices. How about we dig into this and then share what we find?

■ ■ ■

Even if the son in this example goes no further and does no research, there is still value in simply working through impressions, thoughts, opinions, knowledge, and expressing a willingness to learn more. If he *does* decide to do a little research on the relative risks of different jobs, even just those employed by city, state, and federal governments, he might feel better about his friend's choice since garbage collectors, firefighters, crossing guards, and highway maintenance workers all have greater fatal injury rates than police officers in the United States.[6]

Style and Approach

Now that you have four questions for productive conversations with your children, it's time to consider the broader principles that are necessary to show your kids you are interested in their ideas and excited about letting them explore politics with you. Techniques like those in Celeste Headlee's *We Need to Talk: How to Have Conversations That Matter* are invaluable for navigating talks of all kinds, especially political ones. Her work has influenced the way I approach group discussions in class as well as one-on-one talks during office hours.

Having productive conversations isn't a hard thing to do, but it does require some intention. There are four basic pieces that go into this model, and once you've had a few discussions on your own with these in mind, I imagine you'll continue to approach things in this way because conversation turns from something that might be daunting, to something that is delightful. Here are the components to keep in mind:

1. **Curiosity:** Show genuine interest in your teen's political views. Put away distractions and listen actively. Ask clarifying questions without pushing your stance. Use the four previously mentioned questions to guide your inquiry and encourage a two-way exchange.

2. **Biases:** Recognize and reflect on personal biases that may differ from your child's due to varying life experiences. Stay open to these differences during discussions.

3. **Respect:** Treat your teen's opinions with respect. Avoid diminishing their views as naive or something they'll outgrow. Instead, validate their thoughts as worthy contributions to the conversation.

4. **Show You Care:** Make time for in-depth discussions, especially for harder topics. Set ground rules to maintain civility and agree to revisit conversations with fresh perspectives after additional research.

When you are done with a conversation, close it kindly. Thank your child for agreeing to talk with you. Reaffirm your love for them. You will know a good ending when it happens. Both of you may have experienced negative emotions during the conversation, but that loop will be closed with a positive expression of gratitude.

When discussing politics with kids, it's important to choose between open *discussions*—where simply exchanging ideas is the goal—and *debates*—which are aimed at persuading someone or "winning" an argument. Work to recognize your child's conversational preferences: some children enjoy banter and relish the opportunity to showcase their argumentative skills while appreciating the good points made by others. Others will be more interested in acquiring knowledge about a topic without being invested in finding the "right" or "wrong" answer. If you have a child who wants to spar, follow the above guidelines, and conclude with an appreciation for being able to intellectually duke it out with one another. If you have a child who wants to learn more about a subject without necessarily coming to a conclusion, you can do that by agreeing to think about different perspectives without having to render some sort of final judgment.

When talking about politics with kids, it's beneficial to explore the "how"— that is the processes behind political actions and governance. For instance, while news often covers what a law is or its potential impact, it's equally important to discuss how that law came to be and who was involved in the creation and passage of such a law. Questions about how laws are created, how officials are elected, and how judicial decisions are made add depth to a child's understanding of politics. Once you've covered the basic question of what a specific law does, adding in an element of "how" can be a good way to make a larger point about governing have more staying power.

Take a case at the Supreme Court challenging a state law. Coverage might focus on the law's content and consequences of its potential overturn. Yet, discussing how the law was passed, how legislators are chosen, the nature of primaries, districting, and the Supreme Court's case selection process can be another way to add background details to the media story and therefore make the whole topic more engaging to kids. This approach not only informs but also encourages thinking about the structures of our political system and how they can be changed. Hearing the news as what's happening is different than hearing it as what we allow to happen through our system. By connecting our own role to the eventual outcomes of political processes, we begin to show kids about political agency and efficacy. In doing that, they become less accepting of things just being the way they are, and more curious about their role in changing or challenging outcomes they might disagree with.

Complaint Reframing

Think about how sports would be different if all we focused on was how much we hated specific players or coaches from other teams, rather than the celebratory fandom that characterizes most major leagues. We don't find and tell stories to root for in politics—but we could. Parents of different political viewpoints will pick different heroes to share with their kids but focusing on the good versus the bad can go a long way in righting our current discourse.

Stories matter. The way we construct the stories we tell about power and political participation shapes the way our children come to think about politics. If we always come home complaining about politics and just throwing our hands up, our children may feel disempowered and believe the system is inherently negative and unchangeable. While politics can feel frustrating at times, it's important to remember that this isn't always the case. While we may not achieve the desired outcomes immediately, it's the individual people driven to inspire change who can truly make a difference and shape the direction of politics. This holds true for both significant transformations and smaller, everyday changes. Avoid constant complaints about politics at home, which can create a sense of helplessness.

Turn your grievances into learning opportunities by involving your children in discussions about possible improvements and their role in effecting change.

Rather than dwelling on the negatives in politics, make opportunities to celebrate community achievements with your kids. Share stories of local heroes who've positively impacted your community, regardless of their political affiliations. Discuss why you volunteer, highlighting the community impact over partisan politics, to illuminate the human side of civic engagement. Be willing to see the positive parts of politics.

Too often our kids hear us complaining about things, especially in politics. "All politicians are liars," "the city government is so inefficient," "I can't stand our governor" are lines that could be uttered in any one of our homes. And not without reason; a lot of politics can feel like a doom-loop nightmare. If you find *yourself* complaining about the state of politics, use that moment to be a teaching trigger. Ask your kids what they think about the issue or person that's troubling you. Start to do some of that work with them and bring them into your own sorts of questions.

This is a place I will offer specific instruction on what to say. If you find yourself wanting to complain about a certain feature of politics with or around your children, be willing to also ask what could make the point of frustration better. Try to find something that you could do or an idea that you could think about together instead of just complaining. A system is only as good as the abilities of its parts.

When your teens come to you upset about political issues, use the opportunity to broaden the discussion. Ask them what they've heard, think, know, and want to learn about the topic, which helps them move from frustration to understanding and maybe even action. For example, if your teen is upset about the idea of government corruption, explore the topic with them. Ask about their sources, feelings, and understanding, and what they want to learn. Ask what they "know" and how that is possibly different than what they feel or have heard. To really allow them to think about their own agency, instead of simply agreeing that corruption is a problem, ask if there is anything they'd consider doing to advocate for more government transparency. Let them flex their own political muscles by giving them the encouragement to think about what role they could play in fixing a problem.

How Can You and Your Child Find the Same Information to Talk About?

One challenge when discussing issues with children is understanding where they're coming from. Your middle schooler's YouTube content is likely different from the traditional or social media sources you rely on for news. To align your media diets, try a joint digital local newspaper subscription. It may seem daunting but sharing a local newspaper habit where you each agree to read at least one story a week can really energize your concerns and excitement about your community.

When I suggest a subscription to a local paper, I mean one that covers issues that mostly only matter to your town. These subscriptions are generally very cheap; in the town where I spend my summers and weekends, the online subscription is only $3 a month. Local papers' quality varies; some may be ad-heavy, others report community news, while some might lean toward sensationalism. Experimenting with different publications helps you understand your local media landscape.

Local papers have a hard time staying afloat in most media markets as bigger papers or free online content squeezes out a desire for professional coverage. But there really is no better way to be informed about what's happening in a town than by reading a dedicated paper. Subscribing to a local paper not only supports these outlets but also introduces your child to community issues and plants the seed for them to care about whatever town they eventually decide to live in.

Regardless of how you choose to access information, discuss the difference between factual reporting and clickbait with your children. Sharing news sources can bridge gaps, allowing you both to explore common interests and spot biases or misinformation. Many schools have taken up the mantle of developing online information literacy, but it never hurts to have a parent do the same. You'll probably even learn something that you don't already know by asking your kids about how this topic is approached in their school.

Social media is its own beast. It's essential to navigate social media "news" together. So many online, unmoderated platforms can be rife with misleading content. And this content can shape perspectives of people both young and old. By discussing stories and their sources, you can teach your kids to evaluate information in a more rigorous way. At a time when lots of political discussions take place online, talking through issues and sources with your kids will help them both understand things better but also be more able to deploy appropriate skepticism when they encounter stories through these channels.

Dealing with Apathy

Talking to kids about politics doesn't require their constant curiosity; your own active discussions can serve as live examples. If your child isn't inquisitive about politics, they will still learn by observing your engagement. Let them watch you debate local policies with neighbors or see you calling officials to discuss community concerns. For example, if education funding is the local hot topic, let them hear you talk to school board members, exploring budget decisions and their effects on students. This models civic involvement and shows how individuals contribute to policymaking, laying the groundwork for their future participation once an interest or need emerges for them.

Addressing Extremism

When addressing difficult opinions from your child, such as unintentionally or intentionally discriminatory remarks, it's essential to maintain a discussion style that promotes understanding rather than blaming. Listen to their viewpoint, ask about their rationale, and consider rephrasing their statement in a different context. For instance, if they express what might be a biased view about a Muslim class president candidate, you could say, "To make sure I'm understanding, would it be similar to having a prejudiced view of a Catholic candidate with the same goals?" This method helps them see the impact of their views and encourages them to consider broader perspectives.

If your child expresses an opinion that you think is dangerous or veers too close to any sort of extremism, it's important to hear them out still but be firmer and more determined in your style of response. No parent wants to read about their child in the news taking an idea too far or making decisions that put other people at risk. Should your child come to you with extreme views that have elements of violence that concern you, listen but guide the conversation with a firm but open stance. As a parent, you are meant to be the safest space for your kids to explore ideas. It's the role of parents to provide a setting that allows for the constructive moderation of thoughts and actions, and that can only happen if your child feels comfortable in coming to you in the first place. Open dialogue, not confrontation, is key in these moments.

Here are some steps to keep in mind when navigating discussions that hint at extremism:

1. **Open Communication:** Reassure your teen that they can safely express their views at home. Let them know you're ready to listen and not judge.

2. **Engage Actively:** Listen to understand their perspective, not to argue. Use questions to learn more about the reasons behind their opinions.

3. **Express Concerns Calmly:** Share why you find certain ideas worrying. Discuss the values you hold and the possible negative impact of what seem like extremist beliefs. The goal is to do this calmly, rather than in an accusatory way.

4. **Encourage Broader Thinking:** Introduce them to different ideas and viewpoints to put what might be extremism in context. This can be done in a kind way, by trying to use other examples or asking them to think about something from the viewpoint of someone else.

5. **Learn Together:** Research and learn about various viewpoints together. Use resources like books and documentaries to broaden your understanding.

6. **Seek Professional Support:** If your teen's views become increasingly extreme, don't hesitate to consult with a mental health professional experienced in youth and extremism.

Remember, most of your conversations with your child will not go this way, but if they do, it's important to be prepared and approach the situation with understanding. Addressing extremism requires a delicate balance of support and setting clear boundaries. It's essential to seek professional help if you feel your teen's beliefs or behaviors pose a serious threat to themselves or others.

How to Be Heard and Create Change as a Child

Beyond voting, there are so many other ways that we can influence what the different parts of our governments do. *Every person* can call their local council member, state representatives, or federal representatives and weigh in on issues that concern them. Oftentimes you'll just leave a message with a staffer, but these calls add up, weighing on a legislator. If there is a strong and unified position among the constituents in a legislator's district, it can lead to the legislator altering their stance or voting behavior to reflect the will of the people they represent. *Every person* can talk about political or government issues with others who are willing to and can, bit by bit, show their own approach. *Every person* can write to a local paper or start their own sort of protest on issues that really interest them. These are all things we each have the capacity to do if only we prioritize them.

As a mother and a political science professor, I believe in nurturing our children's innate optimism and sense of possibility. Teaching them to channel this energy into meaningful action is one of the most profound lessons we can offer. They learn to appreciate the fruit of steadfast effort over immediate rewards and understand that change is often a marathon, not a sprint. We can all engage in discussions on governance and policy—and we can do more than just talk. Whether it's penning a thoughtful op-ed or spearheading a community demonstration, each of us has the agency to advocate for the issues close to our hearts. It's about making civic engagement a priority, as accessible as it is impactful, for our families and ourselves.

To empower children to make a change, start by identifying the issues that interest or bother them. Encourage them to research these topics, explore different perspectives, and propose their own solutions. Once they've thought of some solutions, help them think about what strategies might be available to them to make real change. Start local and show them how to reach out and communicate effectively. By guiding children through this process, you enable them to develop valuable research skills, learn the importance of civic engagement, and make a positive impact in their communities.

Being an active citizen isn't just about voting. You can take your child to various local events like community board meetings, mayoral "state of the city" addresses, or town hall-style forums. Although these activities may not immediately captivate your child's interest, they effectively demystify and personalize the inner workings of local politics. And many local political offices welcome children as visitors. I make it a point to bring my daughter with me to holiday open houses and other sorts of festive events thrown by my local politicians. If you're able to plan a trip to Washington DC, consider taking your children to the House and Senate galleries to witness our legislators in action or attend oral arguments at the Supreme Court.

Explain to your children the various ways you engage politically, like writing letters or volunteering, and equally, why you might abstain from certain activities. Sharing your reasoning offers them perspective on civic involvement and allows them to think about their own participation. For things that you do that they could also do, such as volunteering or writing letters, offer to do that alongside them.

Reaching Out to Elected Officials

Until now, it's possible that you have never been in touch with an elected or appointed government official and instead have only directly interfaced with government employees at the post office, DMV, or police precinct. Although all these people are important in their executive functions, government employees are different from elected or appointed government officials. Instead of *having* to talk to you, many of them really *want* to talk with you—you've just got to know how to get in contact.

In thinking about government outreach, I suggest that you focus on local- and state-level pathways. Local legislators are those in your city or town council, or for less-populated areas sometimes a committee or board. Local executives are mayors, town executives, or managers. States have legislators who represent each part of the state, and you'll likely just have to get on to your state website to determine who your representatives are. The issues that most affect our day-to-day lives are generally determined at these levels; they are also the most responsive levels of government and far easier to influence through individual or concerted actions.

Mayors and governors themselves can be hard to get in touch with—especially those in charge of areas with larger population sizes. But their administrative offices will have staff who are specifically tasked with community relations who will make themselves available to those seeking a meeting or phone call.

Requesting an in-person meeting or showing up at "office hours" or times held to hear constituent concerns will always be more effective in conveying your message than a phone call, but a phone call will be more effective than an email. For all outreach, the closer and more personal the connection is, the more impactful it will be on the recipient.

A child might want to reach out to someone in local government if they have a concern about the condition of their local park. Let's say the child notices that the playground equipment in the park is damaged, unsafe to use, or just feels run down and outdated compared to other parks.

They can express their concern and ask for repairs with those requests directed to the mayor or the administrative department responsible for parks and recreation. In this case, the child can write a letter or email to the mayor's office or the local parks and recreation department explaining the problem and emphasizing the importance of having a safe and enjoyable park for children in the community. They can also loop in their local representative because the more people in power who are aware of an issue, the greater the chance is that it gets a solution. This child could also offer to volunteer in park cleanup activities on their own or with a group, and then relay those efforts to the officials in charge. But best would be to come in person to deliver the message, with pictures and a letter to leave with the government official.

Local governments can help address concerns like this by taking action to assess the playground equipment, allocate funds for repairs or replacements, and ensure that maintenance is conducted regularly to keep the park safe for children. All of these actions are within the capacities of local government, they likely just come down to funding and prioritization. Local officials may try to involve other community members in the effort—including the original child who brought it to their attention—of park improvement initiatives or seek their input on future park development plans. By reaching out, your child can learn about civic engagement, express their opinions, contribute to making positive changes in their community, and be set up to know more about this sort of policy area in your town moving forward. All of those things are forms of power.

Those in legislative roles are somewhat easier to contact and make connections with. Legislators typically have fewer people in the district or area that they represent. For instance, each of the 51 city council members of New York City is responsible for representing 164,000 people in their districts, while the mayor is tasked with governing all 8.4 million residents. These numbers are lower every other place in the United States, but in all cases, there are fewer constituents represented by an individual legislator than by the executive in that area.

Like executive offices, legislators will typically have at least one staff assistant or intern tasked with interfacing with the public. In some cases, the legislator herself may enjoy connecting with constituents, but in most cases a staff member will be the first point of contact. Don't brush these people aside; anyone willing to do the work of assisting a member of government is generally a capable and willing person in the task of making government better. They also tend to be "people persons" who like feeling helpful to constituents, so get to know interns and assistants, these people not only are invaluable to the legislators themselves, but they can also likely help put you in touch with the people who work on the issues you care about.

Legislators have a different job than executives: they are the people tasked with developing and passing new or replacing old laws. These different responsibilities mean that some complaints or compliments are best directed at executives instead of legislators. If you have an enforcement issue, the first stop is someone in the executive branch, but if you think that's unlikely to change, then head to your legislator and see if there are other mechanisms that can be used to make enforcement more likely.

If you want something to change in the law, such as more money allocated for trash removal, or money for better after-school programs, go to a legislator. Your child might be passionate about sports or outdoor activities and want to advocate for the construction of a new basketball court, skate park, or playground in your neighborhood. They could reach out to their city council member to express their desire for more recreational facilities, and those are the people who can use that feedback to make a proposal or fight for more budget dollars to do just that.

Legislators are far more likely than members of the executive branch of local government to be in spaces that allow for contact with the public. The job and schedule of a legislator means that they often try to be around the public to listen to their ideas and then channel the wishes of their constituents into policy. Legislators do things like hold hearings, roundtables, dedicated question-and-answer sessions, coffee on the corner events, scheduled office hours, and more. If possible, attend one of these events with your child. They might find it boring, but you don't need to make a habit of this—just once should be enough to show them what this sort of role is. Just once allows them to meet the real-life person doing that work. And just once might be enough to get them excited to ask for more opportunities to see government at work.

If you haven't reached out to your local governing officials yet, it's important to figure out how to do so. Don't worry, it's not complicated. A basic online search can help you find who you need to talk to and how to get in touch with them. Just enter "who are my state representatives" in "government of <insert your city or town>," and you'll be on your way to figuring out how things happen where you live and who to talk to. If you can't figure it out on your own, just call the numbers you find associated with any sort of local or state government in your area online and you'll be directed to the right person within a few telephone calls.

I know that might sound like a bit of a pain, but teaching your child to make change is one of the best tools you can give them. Knowing that it takes a little work to figure things out is a good lesson to know. People who do that sort of work are the people who get things done. Kids have a fresh perspective and enthusiasm that can drive powerful outcomes, but they don't know our systems and we can't expect them to figure it out by themselves. These systems are old, are run by older people, and most of the work happens in ways that doesn't look like how they are used to doing school or living life. Along the way, they'll learn about determination and the importance of sustained effort, which are pieces of resiliency—that superpower skill that's related to everything from happiness to success.

Once you have identified who to talk to and how to get in contact with the person you need to in government, let your child know how they can make their effort the most effective:

- Come prepared.
- Use kind and productive language.
- Have a specific ask of the official.
- End the conversation with a positive closing message, thanking the official for their time.

Sometimes these attempts may not result in immediate success. Laws might not change, officials might not respond, or the process might break down. But this is not failure! It's a learning experience that can lead to different approaches in the future. Even if they don't achieve their desired outcome, there will be wins along the way. Most local officials are willing to engage with children who reach out through proper channels, and occasionally your child will be able to bring about the changes they want. Even small steps forward count as victories.

Even if your child isn't particularly interested in making change, there's still value in contacting elected officials. Knowing a real person behind the political role helps them understand that government is tangible and relatable. If your child likes a particular politician, they can become a role model. If they don't take a liking to someone, it helps them think about what kind of political representation they might want in the future.

Getting to know local and state officials is a great way to understand how politics works, and there are no age limits to participate in this manner. If a child knows a local politician, they have a better chance of starting their own petition, collecting signatures from other kids, and even getting coverage in local media. While children may not always be allowed into adult meeting spaces, they can submit their ideas to decision-makers through crafts, recordings, or discussions with a little parental effort.

Knowing and contacting officials is a valuable skill no matter where your child ends up living. The processes may differ, but the basic principles remain the same. Once children realize that government officials are just like anyone else, they'll be less intimidated in the future. They'll feel more connected to the levers of power, ensuring they have avenues for change when they're on their own. Teaching them how to do this while they're still at home is incredibly valuable because both of you are constituents of the same politicians, which may change when they move or go to college.

Petitions

Many times, the ways of doing individual-level politics can be out of reach for children. But if a child knows a local politician, they have a much better route to starting their own petition with signatures from other kids and getting coverage in local media. If you've got a teenager who cares about an issue, telling them about the logistics of a petition or just giving examples of petitions you've heard about should be enough to send them on their way.

I've seen both high schoolers and early college students petition for things from asking their school to reduce plastic use in the cafeteria to advocating for mental health days off from school. I imagine in your community there have been times of teen petitioning as well, so encouraging your teens to research what's been petitioned for in the past can be a way to show them a model of how to do things.

Older children will feel much more comfortable navigating things on their own once you've pushed them in the right direction. Younger children will need more guidance, but they often enjoy doing "grown-up" sorts of things and may delight in getting signatures on their petitions.

Protest

Protest is another option available to children. This is a style of political action that some parents will feel comfortable with, and others may not. Protesting—in accordance with relevant laws—can be an incredibly powerful way to increase coverage of an issue. The overwhelming majority of protests conducted in the United States are peaceful and serve the purposes of uniting a concerned community around a topic by demonstrating strength in numbers. If your child expresses an interest in attending or organizing a protest, but you have never protested yourself, offer to go with them. Older children might not like the idea of their parents tagging along, but for you to be at ease and to be able to debrief on the protest afterward, turning out with them can be a nice option.

Encourage your children to study the approaches of other children and then to share their plans with you. In the 1990s, the media ran stories about how children led the charge in anti-abortion protests.[7] In 2020, 15-year-old Zee Thomas used Twitter (now X) to organize a Black Lives Matter march through her home city of Nashville, Tennessee, with the help of five other teenagers. She had seen coverage of other protests and talked online to other children around her age. The kids agreed to a date and a location and then spread the word through their own networks. Zee Thomas asked her mom for permission and then found herself leading a march of nearly 10,000 people.[8] Around the same time, 17-year-old Tiana Day of San Ramon, California, responded to a post on Instagram and led a Black Lives Matter protest across the Golden Gate Bridge.[9] Our First Amendment protections enshrine the ability of people to protest, and this right extends to our children. Letting them feel that sort of power can be an eye-opening life experience.

Campaigning

Children can actively engage in local politics by organizing and campaigning for candidates, ballot initiatives, or issues they are passionate about. In certain areas, such as in New York City, high school students can even serve as deputy campaign managers in city council races. This role allows them to work alongside experienced individuals and influence campaign strategies. Not only does this provide young people with firsthand exposure to politics, but it also appeals to voters when enthusiastic and well-informed youth engage them on local political matters. The charm and dedication of young campaigners can often sway adults to care more about what is happening in their community.

If you have a high schooler who wants to get involved in a local campaign, encourage them to research the candidates in your area and reach out directly. While they might not become a manager right away, they will gain valuable firsthand experience of what it's like to work on a campaign. This involvement allows them to determine whether they enjoy the excitement and pace of campaign work, which could become a long-term pursuit. Alternatively, if they discover it's not their preferred path, this experience provides them with a valuable lesson about their future aspirations.

Art for Change

In less conventional political action, children can also use the spaces they frequent, such as parks, schools, sidewalks, and libraries, to highlight issues they care about. Armed with a bucket of chalk and some spelling help, even the youngest school-age children can create messages and artwork for those passing by to ponder. Though it might be hard for children to understand their efficacy in the political system that all but excludes them, you can support your kids in finding their own way to communicate their concerns in a public fashion, which at its core is what common politics is all about.

Power and influence don't just have to be about voting or donating. Children can organize friends around specific topics or issues that they care about. They can run fundraisers, create online spaces or events about certain issues, or even mobilize their own letter-writing or protest activities. These sorts of approaches can sometimes be even more beneficial than adult activism since local print, TV, and radio news love to cover stories about concerned kids doing work.

In communities affected by the issue of gun violence in schools, middle and high school students can organize a campaign centered around art and advocacy. They can create powerful works of art, including paintings, sculptures, and posters, that depict their feelings about gun violence and their visions for safer schools. This artwork could be displayed in local galleries and community spaces, drawing attention from both the public and the media.

To better ensure that their ideas reach decision-makers, the students could record video messages discussing their experiences and proposing tangible solutions to prevent gun violence in schools. These videos can be shared on social media platforms and potentially gain significant attention, leading to a groundswell of support from their peers, parents, and concerned community members. Actual change is always harder to implement, but getting the ball rolling is the first step. By showing children how to do this, and equipping them with strategies to make implementation easier, tangible change is that much closer.

In the above example, students can request the creation of a task force consisting of community members, law enforcement, mental health experts, and educators to devise comprehensive strategies for preventing gun violence in schools. This request is relatively easy for a governmental decision-maker to consider.

It Is Necessary That You Do This Work with Your Children

Having conversations with your children about politics is good for so many reasons. You show them that you care. They learn about you. You learn about them. They get to practice conversations in a safe place with you. They start to have impacts on their development in positive ways by learning to advocate for themselves, learning to be resilient, and learning how to adapt and accept positions that they don't hold. They learn the value of following up and how learning more and hard work can pay off.

Research shows that engaging in meaningful discussions helps children express their opinions and emotions later in life.[10] Beginning by introducing political concepts at different stages of their lives, you create a scaffold on which they can build understanding as they get older. Every piece is a little building bock to a robust and working understanding of government, politics, and their role in it. For younger children, focus on the roles of various leaders and the basic functions of government. As they mature, get into more complex issues like elections and legislation, and be willing to learn more on the topics that interest them. The information is all around us; we just have to be willing to seek it and understand.

When difficult topics arise, approach them with honesty and openness. Difficult topics are a part of life; your kids should know this. Show your children how to engage with contentious issues respectfully and thoughtfully, and along the way show them that it's okay to make a mistake and apologize if something hurtful is said. Don't strive for perfection; instead, aim for a conversation environment where questions are encouraged, and it's safe to say "I don't know." The emphasis should be on the exchange itself, not on delivering lectures. They don't need to be U.S. government trivia champions; they need to feel secure in knowing our politics and how they can influence it. Embrace these moments as opportunities for mutual learning and connection—all while building civic capacity for your child. Practicing these conversations will help them develop valuable skills and attitudes like grit that will help them in ways that go beyond politics.

Don't be afraid to experiment with different tools and approaches that work for you and your children. Any conversation is better than avoiding political discussions altogether. In the next part of this book, I go through the things your kids must know to be able to fully participate, and a primer for you to brush up on these subjects yourself.

Notes

1. Zevin, J. (1983). Future citizens: Children and politics. *Teaching Political Science: A Journal of Social Sciences 10* (3): 119–126.
2. Larch, A. (2022), Manchin praises teen for spurring Hurricane skatepark project. *The Herald-Dispatch* (4 November). https://www.timeswv.com/news/west_virginia/manchin-praises-teen-for-spurring-hurricane-skatepark-project/article_340e7978-5c67-11ed-8b4a-97c4df8372bd.html.

3. U.S. Election Assistance Commission. (2020). State-by-state compendium of election worker laws & statutes. https://www.eac.gov/sites/default/files/electionofficials/pollworkers/Compendium_2020.pdf.

4. Giroux, H.A. (2003). *The Abandoned Generation: Democracy Beyond the Culture of Fear*. London: Palgrave Macmillan.

5. Nolas, S.-M., Varvantakis, C., and Aruldoss, V. (2017). Talking politics in everyday family lives. *Contemporary Social Science 12* (1–2): 68–83.

6. Industrial Safety & Hygiene News. (2020). Top 25 most dangerous jobs in the United States (5 November). https://www.ishn.com/articles/112748-top-25-most-dangerous-jobs-in-the-united-states.

7. Banisky, S. (1992). Children lead charge on abortion clinics Corps of devoted youngsters arrested 1 day, back on line next. *The Baltimore Sun* (12 July). https://www.baltimoresun.com/1992/07/12/children-lead-charge-on-abortion-clinics-corps-of-devoted-youngsters-arrested-1-day-back-on-line-next/.

8. Bennet, J. (2020). These teen girls are fighting for a more just future. *The New York Times* (26 June). https://www.nytimes.com/2020/06/26/style/teen-girls-black-lives-matter-activism.html.

9. Martichoux, A. (2020). Tiana Day, teen who led Golden Gate Bridge Black Lives Matter protest, shares how life has changed. ABC 7 News (17 December). https://abc7news.com/black-lives-matter-blm-protests-golden-gate-bridge-protest/8850760/.

10. National Research Council. (2015). Transforming the workforce for children birth through age 8: A unifying foundation.

A Short Primer in U.S. Government: From Understanding to Action

5

What You and Your Kids Need to Know

The remainder of the book is here to provide you with the information you need to get into conversations with your kids about politics and government. While I strive for accuracy, I also include examples to make key points more relatable and understandable. Don't feel pressured to memorize every fact. Use this as a foundation to build upon and find what resonates with you and your children's interest in politics. If something piques the curiosity of your child, don't hesitate to seek further reading and explore more detailed resources. There is no need to quiz yourself or your kids on this content; it's meant to help you better understand things so that you can be a more knowledgeable citizen yourself and better resource for your family.

As you raise your younger and adolescent children, there are two basic things to keep in the back of your mind in how you approach politics with them. First, you must recognize your role—both as the person your kid will come to when they want to know something, and the person they unwittingly take after in how you approach political discussions—and you need to consider restraint in your negative assessments of politics. Second—and perhaps the one that will take the most effort on your part—is to research and reach out to at least one local, state, or federal elected official and introduce your child to them. By humanizing politics, you go a long way in the effort to demystify politics to your kids.

Before venturing out on their own, there are five essential civic skills every child should learn to be prepared to be a participating citizen. The first is navigating challenging discussions, a skill that comes with practice and grows with the guidance of a knowledgeable parent—a theme we've already touched upon in the previous chapters. The remaining four skills are centered on gaining practical know-how of politics and government. The rest of the book is a primer on politics and government, written so that you may reacquaint yourself with the pieces of civic education that you might not have encountered since high school—or maybe ever! Though I give thorough treatments of the civic skills your kids ought to have in the remainder of the book, here is a preview of these five skills:

1. **How to Have Difficult Conversations:** As our children become young adult citizens, they need to be equipped with the skills to engage in respectful discussions, ask meaningful questions, listen to others' perspectives, and find common ground on political topics. By doing this work with your children, they will be practiced and better able to talk about political subjects and work to influence government for the rest of their lives

2. **Voting:** Voting is a fundamental right and responsibility of every citizen. Active citizens must know how to register and stay current with voter registration. Procedures vary by state, so staying informed is necessary to ensure young adults can participate in the democratic process.

3. **Primaries and General Elections:** It's important to understand that elections happen at various levels, and primary elections can have a significant impact on the outcome. In many places sometimes the only election that determines a winner happens during the primary, not the general election.

4. **Constitutional Knowledge:** Basic understanding of the government's structure, the separation of powers, and constitutional rights is key to informed citizenship. It surprises my students, but really, once you understand this document, a lot of things you encounter in the media will make sense, not enrage you.

5. **Federalism:** Knowledgeable citizens appreciate that politics isn't just national; state and local governance is equally important. Understanding federalism helps young voters better understand how to address things in their communities.

The rest of this chapter serves as a quick guide to some basic governmental concepts and practices. Having these in the back of your mind will help contextualize why our government works the way it does.

■ ■ ■

The federal and state constitutions lay down the rules of our government. Mastering every law and rule is an impossible task, but in learning the basic principles and concepts that form the core of our governance, you'll be much better equipped to understand who does what at government levels. Think of this section as a map to help you on a greater navigation challenge. By understanding the major routes and street grid, you can get quite close to your target location. Once you have the address of a specific destination to head toward, you can do more detailed research to get to the exact answer. That's pretty much what politics is anyhow, a bunch a basic things that are all made unique by determining the specifics.

The core principles guiding our democracy aren't codified laws but rather enduring norms that have shaped governance since America's founding over 230 years ago. These principles both propel and sometimes slow down our system. The founders structured a democratic republic to improve efficiency over previous systems, while deliberately incorporating checks and balances to prevent rash changes possible in autocracies or monarchies. The broader principles that I cover are democratic republicanism, citizen participation, popular sovereignty, separation of powers, checks and balances, and the rule of law with equal application.

In this chapter, I go over those principles and then outline a few governmental basics so that when your child comes to you, you'll have some answers at the ready. As always, no one can know all of this, so feel good about saying that you're going to learn some things together with your children.

Democratic Republicanism

Debating whether the United States is a democracy *or* republic is foolish—it's a democratic republic, incorporating elements of both systems. Democracy involves translating the will of people to an outcome by asking the people directly and using the majority response to come to a decision. In all our elections except for the presidential election—which uses the electoral college—voters' choices are democratically translated into winners. In Congress, majority votes determine what becomes law. In our courts, majorities decide the fates of defendants.

Republicanism is where a few people represent or act on behalf of the many. Our republicanism means we choose representatives to make decisions on our behalf, which is necessary in a country of 330 million people. This republican element allows for efficient policymaking by deferring decisions to those we elect. Democratic principles focus on selection by majority will, while republican principles focus on policy implementation by elected representatives.

When casting both ideals historically, the notion of *citizenship* is very important. Initially, the right to participate in both the democratic and republican elements of our government government—both in voting and holding office—was restricted largely to land-owning white men above a certain age. This did not negate the existence of a democracy but indicated a democracy with tightly held reins, where only a select few had the power to determine eligibility for citizenship and, by extension, participation in governance.

It's necessary to acknowledge explicitly that during the founding of the United States, the institution of slavery was a reality. Enslaved African Americans were denied all rights of citizenship and personhood. They were not recognized as citizens and had no voice in the democracy that was being shaped. Similarly, women were also excluded from the democratic process. They did not gain the right to vote nationwide until the Nineteenth Amendment was passed in 1920.

Major movements in U.S. history have consistently pushed toward expanding the franchise—which is a short way of saying, the right to vote. The abolition of slavery, the women's suffrage movement, the Civil Rights Movement, and the ongoing fight for the rights of immigrants and other groups have all been part of the broader endeavor to widen the scope of who is considered a citizen and who can participate in the democratic process of the United States.

Citizen Participation and Popular Sovereignty

A true democracy relies on the active engagement and decision-making of its citizens. Yet, historically, "people" didn't equate to all individuals within a society; the founders reserved political participation for "citizens," initially a narrow group of privileged men. They sought to replace the hereditary power of monarchies with citizen-based governance, broadening who could wield and hold political power, though clearly in ways that kept many people outside of formal *citizen participation*.

The founders aimed for *popular sovereignty*, where the governed have a significant say in government composition and operation. This philosophy of self-rule is central to our governance, eschewing hereditary titles and ensuring any citizen can participate in government without needing royal familial lineage. In fact, our founding documents clearly state that no U.S. citizen seeking a government position may accept royal titles from any other country.

Power derived from the consent of the governed—championed by thinkers like Thomas Paine—highlighted the shift from hereditary rule to a government based on the will of its people. This founding principle of the United States was radical at the time but has since readily spread as hundreds of democracies based on popular sovereignty have emerged around the world.

However, the practical application of popular sovereignty and inclusive citizenship initially fell short of these ideals. The founders' caution against too much public influence led to a restricted political landscape, initially open only to wealthy white men of European descent. The process of expanding the politically eligible population in the United States has been gradual and often contentious.

First, the franchise expanded beyond the wealthy elite to include more white men, regardless of their wealth. Subsequent legal and constitutional changes, particularly after the Civil War, aimed to extend voting rights to men of all racial backgrounds, though in practice, various mechanisms were used to disenfranchise African American men. The suffrage movement, which gained traction in the late-nineteenth and early-twentieth centuries, resulted in women securing the right to vote with the ratification of the Nineteenth Amendment in 1920. Later expansions of the electorate included granting voting rights to residents of Washington DC, who had previously been excluded from federal elections, and the lowering of the voting age from 21 to 18 with the ratification of the Twenty-sixth Amendment in 1971, in part a response to arguments that if 18-year-olds could be drafted to fight in wars, they should also be able to vote.

The evolution of America's politically eligible population has been a complex journey toward ever greater inclusion, continuously pushing the boundaries of who is considered a rightful participant in our democracy.

Popular sovereignty extends beyond voting; it's manifested in various forms of civic engagement. By casting ballots, signing petitions, running for office, or serving in the military, citizens actively shape their government. Furthermore, registered voters may participate in grand juries, evaluating if enough evidence exists to indict someone, and petit juries, who decide verdicts in trials—necessary roles in the justice system.

Registering to vote unlocks forms of citizenship, but our young people are far less likely to be registered than any other age group. In the 2020 elections, roughly 40% of 18- to 24-year-olds were not registered, compared to just 20% of voters aged 65–74.[1]

Americans must actively maintain voting eligibility. Voter registration, often a complex process requiring proof of identity and residency, isn't a one-time event but an ongoing responsibility, particularly after moving or changing one's name. Although popular sovereignty and civic participation are foundational to our democracy, realizing these ideals means citizens must proactively engage and re-engage in the electoral process. It's critical, especially for our young people, to understand the significance of voter registration, as representative self-governance depends on our participation.

Separation of Powers

Our government's power is distributed across different branches to prevent any single entity from having too much control. This structure, recognized for its benefits since colonial times, consists of three distinct branches: legislative, executive, and judicial.

The legislative branch—Congress—has the authority to draft and enact laws. Directly elected legislators have the responsibility for shaping the laws we abide by. While the Constitution is the ultimate authority, Congress can enact laws that remain valid unless challenged or repealed. Besides legislating, Congress has roles in oversight, investigation, and budget management. Known as "the power of the purse," Congress can raise taxes and fund initiatives it deems necessary. Similarly, state and local governments hold legislative powers to address the unique needs of their communities.

Executive power, vested in the president and the executive branch, is to implement and enforce laws enacted by Congress. This includes discretion in law enforcement prioritization; for example, the federal government may defer action on marijuana use in states where it's legal, focusing instead on combating international drug trafficking. Executive orders, a form of administrative power, can direct actions within the federal government, such as increasing federal employment for people with disabilities, but don't extend to private or state entities. State and local governments have their own executive branches, headed by governors and mayors, respectively, which enforce state and local laws.

Judicial power enables courts to interpret laws and review the constitutionality of legislative and executive actions. Courts respond to challenges, rather than proactively assessing laws or actions for constitutional conflicts. And, of course, states have their own courts systems as well.

In short, Congress legislates or sets the rules of the game, the executive branch executes or administers the rules, and the courts come into play when there is a question with either the rules in the first place or about enforcement. This is the structure of our federal system and is replicated, with slight modifications, at the state and local levels.

Checks and Balances

Checks and balances are our system's safeguards, ensuring no single government branch wields too much power. Each branch can "check" the others, maintaining a balanced distribution of authority.

The legislative branch creates laws, influencing the other branches that are subject to these laws. While the judiciary can advocate for more resources, its existence and structure depend on legislative decisions. Similarly, the executive can only operate agencies that Congress has authorized.

If you were to think about U.S. democracy as a game, the Constitution would be the rule book, the legislative branch would write additional "house rules" consistent with the rule book, the executive branch would execute and enforce the rules, and the judicial branch would weigh in when someone alleges either that the "house rules" are faulty in contrast to the Constitution or when two or more parties have different interpretations of the rules.

The executive branch can check legislative power through presidential vetoes, where the president can reject legislation passed by Congress. Although Congress can override this veto with a two-thirds majority, which is a higher threshold than the usual majority vote, it's a rare occurrence. Additionally, the executive branch exerts influence over how laws are enforced, with each administration prioritizing certain policies over others, which can be a "check" to a Congress that passes a law that the executive doesn't wish to enforce.

Judicial checks on the legislative branch occur when courts rule on the constitutionality of laws. Courts do not automatically review every law, but if one is challenged, they hold the power to invalidate any law or its parts that are found unconstitutional.

The legislative branch can override a presidential veto, with both chambers needing to agree. It also checks the executive through its control of the federal budget, with the power to fund or defund programs as a way to assert its priorities. This dynamic is more pronounced when the president and the congressional majority are from opposing parties. Congress also can control the salary of the president, although not during the current term of a president; rather they must pass laws that dictate the salary of the next presidential term to apply to whoever fills that role.

Additionally, the Senate exercises special checks on the executive, particularly regarding appointments and international agreements. Presidential nominations for executive positions and federal judgeships require Senate confirmation, so presidents must pick candidates who a majority of the Senate is willing to support.

In foreign policy, while the president can take initial military action without Congress's consent, they must keep Congress informed. All military engagements beyond initial actions require congressional approval. The Senate must also ratify treaties. Although the president's international policing powers expanded post-9/11 through an Authorization of Use of Military Force agreed to by Congress, Congress still has the exclusive authority to declare war.

The House and Senate also share responsibility for the check of impeachment, or the power to remove an executive from office. The House initiates impeachment proceedings to charge an executive, while the Senate conducts the trial and votes on the outcome. This process also applies to federal judges.

The judicial branch checks the executive by reviewing the constitutionality of its actions when challenged in court.

The judiciary is subject to multiple checks: the executive appoints judges, Congress defines their jurisdiction and sets their compensation, and the Senate confirms appointments. While judges receive protection from pay decreases and cost-of-living increases during their term, as affirmed in *Beer v. United States*, they can still be counterbalanced. The executive can override judicial decisions through pardons, and Congress can revise laws following court rulings to align with judicial interpretations. These checks, while sometimes indirect, ensure a balance of power among the branches.

The three-part structure of our government, with its system of checks and balances, ensures stability and deliberate policy-making. While this can sometimes result in perceived inefficiency, it guards against rapid policy shifts and aligns with the framers' intent for a cautious evolution of laws that reflects the collective will over time.

The Rule of Law and Equality in Application

The rule of law is the principle that written, universally applicable laws should govern society, not the arbitrary decisions of those in power. This is fundamental in a democratic republic, where laws are created publicly and meant to be applied equally to everyone. By having an independent judiciary that is separate from other government branches and appointed for life, our system is supposed to preserve and uphold the rule of law and ensure fair, unbiased judicial decisions.

These principles of rule of law and judicial independence bring stability and predictability, enabling informed decisions by clarifying legal boundaries and consequences. This concept is akin to household rules that, when clearly communicated, are more likely to be followed and understood by children, promoting order and understanding of consequences for not adhering to them.

In recent years, there have been growing concerns about the independence of the judicial branch and its potential ties to political operatives. And these concerns are not without merit. The courts are still a political branch; they are appointed by the president and confirmed by the Senate. Democratic presidents tend to pick Democratic judges and Republican presidents tend to pick Republican judges. It is not a system that is perfectly insulated from politics, because that is not possible. It's one that has more guardrails than other parts of our politics, so the courts are not a nonpolitical branch, but instead thought of as the least political branch. Concerns about political influence in the courts have led to current fights and initiatives aimed at safeguarding the courts' autonomy and preserving the rule of law. It's a tricky thing to figure, as the courts want to self-police by creating their own ethical guidelines, but members of Congress too want to make sure there are laws governing how judges can and cannot comport themselves.

Conclusion

Understanding the foundational elements of our government, such as the basic principles, the electoral processes, constitutional knowledge, and the value of federalism, allows us to better engage with our nation's political workings. Once you understand more about our politics and government, you'll be better able to guide your children through the complexities of governance and encourage them to participate in democracy. Now that we've got a few fundamentals down, let's get into one of the most consequential things your children need to know how to do: how to vote and navigate elections.

Note

1. U.S. Census Bureau. (2020). Current population survey (November).

6

Voting and Navigating Elections

Teaching your child *how* to vote may be the single most important thing you teach them in their political lives. Not so much because an individual vote is powerful, but because this is the essential connective piece between each one of us and the government we consent to be governed by. A person who is a voter is a person who knows a little bit more, cares a little bit more, and matters a lot more in our political system.

In the summer of 2020, with the pandemic altering life's rhythm, I found a teachable moment with my daughter about the importance of voting. Our kitchen table, scattered with campaign flyers, became our classroom. As we faced the challenges of a COVID-affected election, I shared with her the role voting plays in shaping our government. Although the pandemic meant she couldn't join me at the polls this time, the experience deepened our ongoing conversation about civic duty. Through discussions and active participation, I have aimed to inspire her to appreciate her future role as a voter, emphasizing the community benefits and personal fulfillment that come from participating in democracy. And I do make a point to bring her to the polls every time I can.

By actively involving your children in the voting process, you increase the likelihood that they will become voters themselves. That's why civic groups encourage people to bring their children to the polls and governments distribute "Future Voter" stickers. Experiencing the physical act of voting and receiving a small reward like a sticker creates a positive connection with the process. When you vote, take your child with you.

Teaching your child the value of voting can have far-reaching effects. Voting enriches both personal and community well-being, making it a powerful habit to pass on to your children. Multiple studies show that voting is habit-forming *and* contagious.[1] Studies suggest that voters are more likely to be community-minded, engaging in activities like volunteering and donating to charity.[2] They often encourage others to participate in civic duties as well, helping to create a bigger community of active citizens.[3] Moreover, voters tend to report better overall health.[4] By promoting a voting culture at home, you not only bolster your family's civic responsibility but also contribute to the broader societal good.

How to Register to Vote

In the United States, the right to vote is generally granted to citizens who are at least 18 years old, have a permanent address, are not currently incarcerated, have not been declared mentally incompetent by a court, *and* have registered to vote. This right is impacted by felony convictions in some states—everywhere except Vermont, Maine, and Washington DC voting age citizens convicted of a felony are not allowed to vote for at least some period of time.[5] In all states except North Dakota, voter registration is a prerequisite for electoral participation. Since schools may not adequately cover how to register to vote in the remaining 49 states, parents should ensure their teens are prepared to navigate the system.

Many people anticipate voter registration to be cumbersome, but it's often straightforward—more akin to checking in for a doctor's appointment than navigating DMV procedures. It's not an easy thing to do, but it's not particularly difficult either—it's just something to figure out and get done. Guide your teen through registration when they're eligible and remind them to update their registration whenever they move. These are simple little things that will stay with them for life.

Voter registration requirements vary across states, with some allowing same-day registration on Election Day, while others require registration 10–30 days in advance. I wish I could write all the details here, but states vary so much, and things change, so looking this up on your own will be the best thing to do. The official government website of your state is the go-to resource. You can find it by searching for "your state name" followed by "voter registration" on your preferred search engine. State websites vary in terms of layout and accessibility, but with a little exploration, you'll discover the information you need to get registered no matter where you live.

In certain states, registering with a political party is required to vote in party primaries, though this is not a rule everywhere. In states where one party is dominant, participating in primaries may be the "real" election for influencing the general election outcome, making party registration important if you want to have an impact on selecting who will likely go on to win a general election.

How to Register: Many, but not all, states offer online voter registration. This is like making a purchase or signing up for something online. All states offer in person or mail-in registration. You can figure out how things work in your state by going to your state's government website.

When to Register: States use different deadlines for voter registration. Timing is usually some number of days before the next election to be eligible to participate. Deadlines to register span between 0 and 30 days before an election, depending on your state. When kids move out of state for school or work, it's likely that they'll face a difference election registration deadline than they do in your state—this is why knowing about these sorts of things is important before a child leaves your home. The whole voter registration process can be hard to navigate and is highly variable, but without registering to vote, citizens can't participate, so it's a critical piece to work through with your kids.

Information to Register: States determine what sorts of information voters must provide to be eligible to vote. Like the deadlines, these vary as well. To ensure a smooth registration process, prepare all necessary documents in advance. Generally, you'll need identification such as a driver's license or Social Security number. It's a good idea to have these documents handy when you start the registration process. When your child does this for the first time, help them collect their information, as this might be the first time they've interacted with these sorts of documents themselves.

Preregistration: Preregistration allows teens to prepare for voting before turning 18. Some states allow preregistration at 16, others at 17, and a few have different age requirements. Additionally, many states permit registration for those who will be 18 by the next election. Check your state's voter registration rules to guide your teen through this process.

Some states permit 17-year-olds to vote in primaries if they'll be 18 by the general election, enabling them to influence candidate selection early on. For current voter registration details, the National Conference of State Legislatures website at ncsl.org and the federal site vote.gov are reliable resources, with the latter offering a state-by-state guide.

How to Vote

Voting procedures, including ID requirements, early and online voting, and absentee ballot rules, differ by state. It's important to learn the specific voting and registration processes for your state.

Where to Vote: Polling places, which can be located in community centers, schools, or other public spaces, differ by state. You've got to know your designated precinct or polling station. Voting at the incorrect location could lead to using a provisional ballot, which might need extra steps to be counted in the final total. Information about polling sites is available on state government websites. Always verify your polling site before going to cast a ballot, as locations can change due to redistricting or voter registration updates. Check the location and hours of your polling station a week in advance to ensure a hassle-free voting day. Encourage your kids to do the same when they first do this on their own.

When to Vote: Voting methods also differ by state, with all offering some combination of in-person voting on Election Day, early voting, and mail-in or absentee voting. Eight states and Washington DC, mainly use mail voting but also provide early in-person options. Forty-six states, DC, and three territories offer early, in-person or mail voting for all people, with some states starting up to 50 days before an election, but usually lasting 10–20 days and often ending a few days before Election Day. Weekend voting availability varies by state.

All states have a combination of in-person voting and mail-in or absentee voting, and all permit voters to make a choice as to how they'll cast a ballot, but eligibility for mail in or absentee balloting depends on state law. Research the options available in your area and choose the method that works best for you. If your child leaves for college, help them register to vote at their new address. They will be spending the majority of their time at that location, it will be easier to vote in person than absentee, and they'll be able to connect to the local politics of where they currently live, versus where they used to live. There is a consideration of timeliness, in that most elections happen in the fall, shortly after college orientation, so make sure to talk about registration details early and make sure they square things away in time to be eligible to vote.

What to Bring – Voter Identification: Voter ID requirements vary by state. Some states require photo ID such as a driver's license or passport, while others accept non-photo ID like utility bills, bank statements, birth certificates, Medicare or Medicaid identification cards, hunting or fishing licenses, concealed handgun carry licenses, pilot's licenses, health insurance cards, paychecks, property tax statements, vehicle insurance card, college identifications, or other documents. First-time voters might face additional ID requirements, but established voters often need fewer documents. In some states, like New York, voters may only need to confirm their identity and sign a form before voting. Always check what's needed before heading to the polls.

Preparing to Vote—Talk It Out with Your Kids!

When preparing to vote, it's helpful to look at a sample ballot beforehand. You can usually find these online on your state's website, and some states mail these out to registered voters ahead of time. If your state does this, you might receive a mailing with details about each candidate and position. If not, you can find this information on third-party websites like ballotpedia.org. Taking the time to familiarize yourself with the candidates and positions beforehand can make you feel more confident and prepared when you enter the polling station. Of course, for many people— even the most politically involved—this can be an overwhelming task because there are elections for so many positions. There will be elections where you go to vote and are caught unaware of the names or even the positions on the ballot. This happens to everyone and shouldn't make you feel like you're not a good participant in the process. It shows you that there's a place for you to try to learn a little bit more next time around.

Reviewing the candidates and positions doesn't have to be overwhelming; in fact, it can be an enjoyable activity to do as a family. You can discuss the candidates together, sharing your thoughts on who you believe would be a good fit and why. It's a chance to engage in meaningful conversations and consider what qualities you value in politicians and what expectations you have for those seeking office. This is one of my favorite things to do with my daughter. Going through the candidate lists and discussing their platforms allows us to make informed decisions and think about who we want to represent us. It's a valuable exercise to think independently and form our own opinions rather than relying solely on media or peer influence.

Primaries Versus General Elections

Now that we have a grasp of the basics of voting, let's consider two types of elections you will encounter: primaries and general elections. Knowing the difference between primary and general elections is another piece of information your children should know before they leave your home. In most states, there are *primary* elections where political parties hold contests to determine their candidates for the final, *general* election. Primary elections are contests within a specific party to pick a nominee who will then go on to contest other nominees from other parties. Though the elections are within parties, they are still conducted by state and municipal governments—not the parties themselves.

In some states, primary elections are "closed" meaning voters must be registered with a specific party to participate. Only registered members of that party are allowed to cast their ballot. "Open" primaries allow any registered voter to participate in any party's primary without declaring a party affiliation. This allows voters to privately choose which party's primary they want to participate in, regardless of their party affiliation or lack thereof. There are also systems where party-unaffiliated voters can participate in a party's primary, while registered party members can only vote in their respective party's primary. No matter the state system, each voter is permitted to participate in only one primary.

California and Washington have a "top two" primary system where all candidates, regardless of party, compete together. The top two vote-getters advance to the general election, even if from the same party. Louisiana's system allows all candidates into the general election, with a run-off between the top two if no one gets over 50% of votes.

Primaries tend to have significantly lower turnout than general elections despite the fact that they are sometimes the only election that matters for the eventual general election outcome. Primaries are especially pivotal in areas with a large majority of voters supporting one party.

Let me give you an example from my home state of New York. In certain districts of New York City, the voter registration ratio between Democrats and Republicans can be as much as 75% to 25%. This trend is even more pronounced in other areas or smaller localities. Consequently, during the general election, regardless of the Republican Party's nominee, their chances of winning against a Democrat are slim due to the sheer number of registered Democrats who typically lean toward supporting Democratic candidates in general elections. As a result, the *real* competition for representation occurs much earlier during the primary election, where multiple candidates vie for the opportunity to secure the party nomination. Those participating in the primary understand that this is the election that will determine the ultimate outcome in the overall election. I encourage all of my friends who want to participate in our elections to register with a party—as I do to others who live in other closed primary states.

It's important to understand the role of primary elections beyond the well-known presidential primaries. Primaries determine party candidates for all levels of general elections, a fact not emphasized in high school civics. Equipping your children with this knowledge ensures they can fully participate and influence election outcomes. Look up the election laws in your state. Understand if you are in an open or closed primary system. Consider what that means for you when you register to vote and whether or not you might be better served registering with a party. As you figure these things out for yourself, let your kids in on what you determine.

Federal, State, and Local Elections

The United States holds thousands of elections annually, with states overseeing the process no matter if it's a federal, state, or local election. While federal election dates are consistent, local and state elections use different, state-specific dates. All House seats are up for reelection every two years, which can coincide with the presidential election or occur during *midterm elections*, representing the midway point of a presidential term. Senate elections also take place every two years, but only one-third of the Senate is eligible for election in any given election cycle due to the staggered six-year terms of that chamber. While the "highest vote getter" method is most common, some states use ranked choice voting for federal elections or runoffs if no candidate gets a majority.

State and local elections are very similar to federal elections, they are conducted in the same places, use the same machinery, and ballots will look the same. But election timings, term lengths, and term limits differ by state. State and local elections also sometimes differ from federal ones, with unique rules like voting rights for under-18s or noncitizen residents in some local elections. Local and state elections far outnumber federal ones, with positions from school boards to law enforcement. These roles can affect education, justice, and more; though they garner less media coverage, they really do impact quality of life things faced by everyday people. And though they are more consequential for day-to-day life, state and local elections have far lower turnout than federal elections.

The Presidential Election

Presidential elections often leave a lasting impression on young people due to their prominence in media. These elections are unique, as no other office is selected with the input of people from all states. Though high profile, the multi-month nomination process and the workings of the Electoral College are oftentimes fuzzy—even for experienced voters.

The Democratic and Republican parties select their presidential nominees through state primaries and caucuses, which occur on different dates and under different rules throughout the states. Candidates gain support proportionate to the votes they secure in these state primaries and caucuses. These party-specific elections end with nominating conventions before the November general election and the procedures for each party are based on tradition and party norms rather than constitutional mandate.

Primaries allow voters to vote for their preferred presidential candidate through ballots, similar to general elections. Caucuses are interactive party meetings where members debate, discuss, and select a candidate through public voting, such as a show of hands or walking to a corner of a room to show how many supporters each candidate has. Caucus voting can include several rounds where participants may realign to support more popular candidates and less popular ones are eliminated.

States may use primaries, caucuses, or a mix of both, with specific rules varying by state and party. Again, you've got to research your state's process for details. States decide how to run their primaries or caucuses but coordinate with national parties on timing. States like Iowa and New Hampshire typically hold the first caucuses and primaries and can significantly impact the race due to their early positions and media attention.

In presidential primaries and caucuses, voters are actually choosing delegates committed to specific candidates to represent them at national nominating conventions, not the individual candidates themselves, though candidate names will appear on ballots. The state parties decide the number of delegates, with potential adjustments determined by the national party. Voting in primaries typically binds delegates to their pledged candidates.

Some states allocate all delegates to the leading candidate, while others divide delegates proportionally based on vote share. Both major parties also have unpledged delegates, with the Democratic Party's being known as superdelegates, who can support any candidate.

National conventions, while still pivotal, now function more as formal affirmations of candidates and campaign launches. At these events, delegates finalize the party platform, defining the party's objectives and policy positions, which influence the campaign and political direction.

The Electoral College is a system used in the United States *only* to determine the president and vice president. Instead of tallying individual votes nationwide, it counts electors by state. Each state's elector count equals its congressional representation. For instance, California had 55 electors in 2020 because it has 53 representatives and 2 senators. All states have a minimum of three electors and Washington DC also has three electors, despite lacking full congressional representation, because the Twenty-third Amendment provided the capital city with the number of electors equal to the number of electors granted to the least populous state. The number of electors each state has can change with each Census, when the total number of representatives apportioned to each state changes.

For the Electoral College, most states use a winner-take-all approach, where the candidate with the most votes earns all that state's electors. To appreciate how this works consider Pennsylvania in 2020. Even though the 2020 election was close in that state, with a difference of only 80,555 votes favoring Joe Biden over Donald Trump, all 20 electors from Pennsylvania went to the Biden who won the popular vote in the state.

When these sorts of close elections deliver all of the electoral votes to one candidate we sometimes find ourselves in a situation where one candidate earns more individual votes than electoral votes, meaning that more people in the United States preferred one candidate for president, but in the way that votes are aggregated, the Electoral College determines a different outcome. To win the presidency, a candidate must gain at least 270 of the 538 total Electoral College votes. In 2016, the candidate who did that was Donald Trump, winning 304 Electoral College votes to Hillary Clinton's 227, even though Clinton earned 65,853,625 individual votes to Trump's 62,985,106 votes.

Concluding Thoughts

Understanding the basics of voter registration and the specific voting procedures in our states is imperative for active participation in the political process. By giving your children the knowledge and tools to navigate the complexities of voter registration, you empower them to make their voices heard. By teaching our children about the significance of primary elections, we prepare them with the understanding needed to actively participate in shaping the political landscape. And what's better is that none of this is hard to do. You figure out far more difficult systems in the course of being an adult, like health insurance or getting a mortgage—learning a few dates, figuring out if you have open or closed primaries, and showing up to cast a ballot are totally doable things. And once you know how to do this, you can pass that on to your kids and they'll be forever more powerful because you showed them the way.

Happy voting!

Notes

1. Nickerson, D.W. (2008). Is voting contagious? Evidence from two field experiments. *American Political Science Review 102* (1): 49–57; Zelizer, A. (2019). Is position-taking contagious? Evidence of cue-taking from two

field experiments in a state legislature. *American Political Science Review 113* (2): 340–352; De Rooij, E.A., Green, D.P., and Gerber, A.S. (2009). Field experiments on political behavior and collective action. *Annual Review of Political Science 12*: 389–395.

2. Gerber, A.S., Green, D.P., and Shachar, R. (2003). Voting may be habit-forming: Evidence from a randomized field experiment. *American Journal of Political Science 47* (3): 540–550.

3. Marschall, M.J. (2004). Citizen participation and the neighborhood context: A new look at the coproduction of local public goods. *Political Research Quarterly 57* (2): 231–244.

4. Denny, K.J. and Doyle, O.M. (2007). ". . . Take up thy bed, and vote." Measuring the relationship between voting behaviour and indicators of health. *The European Journal of Public Health 17* (4): 400–401.

5. In fact, in Vermont, Maine, and DC, incarcerated people can vote while serving time in custody, though very few actually do. Lewis, N. (2019). In just two states, all prisoners can vote. Here's why few do. The Marshall Project. https://www.themarshallproject.org/2019/06/11/in-just-two-states-all-prisoners-can-vote-here-s-why-few-do.

7

The Constitution

The Constitution can be thought of as our charter of government. It spells out who can do what and outlines the principles and structures upon which the U.S. government operates. Reading the Constitution is a civic exercise that I require my students to do and encourage everyone to do. In understanding the document, you'll better understand the roles of government, your rights within our system, and how to better participate in our democracy. Though detailed, it's surprisingly short. It's not the sort of document to read and digest in a day—though you certainly could read it all in a day—but going through it with your kids can be an activity that you do together over years. Once you get into reading it, the questions they'll have—and those that you will probably have—can be the foundation of a number of engaging conversations and little research sessions together.

In my introductory classes, we take two weeks to go over the Constitution, covering its seven articles across four lessons.

Some articles are trickier than others, but there's no rush—you and your kids can take as much time as you need at home.

Introducing the Constitution's concepts can be fun for younger kids, who love learning about rules through games and activities. Think of it as explaining the "rules" of how our country works—though you'll have to modify the language so that they can better understand things. For teens, reading and discussing the Constitution can be a deep dive into our nation's foundations. If you really get into it, you could make it interactive with a family quiz night.

In this chapter, I start with an overview of the Constitution, explaining the central parts before moving on to the amendments. For each article, I've created a small summary with five key things to takeaway. Discussions on amendments come with conversation prompts to kick-start talks with your kids, and I'll suggest extra materials for those who want to learn more. I do not reproduce the Constitution here, though there are many outlets online that do.[1]

The Origins of the Constitution

The U.S. Constitution, drafted in 1787 and enacted in 1788, replaced the Articles of Confederation to create a stronger federal government. It was crafted by lawyers, merchants, and plantation owners, who initially aimed to amend the Articles but ended up forming a new government. Influenced by state constitutions, it established a federal system with a careful balance of power.

The Constitution's authors had differing ideas about government's role, which were deliberated for weeks and resulted in compromises. Central debates included the extent of federal power and the contentious issue of slavery. These discussions are detailed in historical records and the drafters' personal writings, available through the Library of Congress.[2]

There are seven articles in the Constitution, each focused on a different topic:

Article 1 – The Legislative Branch

Article 2 – The Executive Branch

Article 3 – The Judicial Branch

Article 4 – The States

Article 5 – Amendments

Article 6 – Debts, Supremacy, Oaths

Article 7 – Ratification

Article 1 – The Legislative Branch

The first—and longest—article of the Constitution establishes the legislative branch of Congress. There's debate about why it's first. Some think it underscores Congress as the foremost branch; others say it's to ensure the legislative powers are defined before the executive, avoiding an overly dominant president.

The Federal Convention needed Congress to transmit this new document to the states for ratification, making it necessary to establish the powers and structure of the legislative branch. Plus, many at the convention anticipated better odds of being elected to Congress than becoming president or a Supreme Court justice, so they naturally focused on the legislative details. Back then, the executive branch was seen as secondary to the legislature's central role.

Our federal legislative branch is called Congress, which consists of two chambers: the House of Representatives and the Senate. Representatives are directly elected by citizens every two years for two-year terms, while one-third of the Senators are elected every two years for six-year terms. This means that every two years all 435 representatives are up for reelection, and 33 or 34 senators are also up for reelection. Representatives have always been elected directly, while senators were originally chosen by state legislatures until the Seventeenth Amendment introduced direct elections for senators in 1913. The idea that the House of Representatives must all face reelection was meant to promote some turnover in the ranks. In the Senate, the staggered terms mean that two-thirds of the Senate will remain in place during the possible transition of the entire House and one-third of the Senate. That continuity is meant to keep some institutional knowledge intact. In practice, most—meaning over 90%—of sitting representatives and senators who run for reelection win.

To determine the population of each state, a national Census is conducted every 10 years—the most recent one took place in 2020. Initially, the enumeration of people in the United States for the Census was determined by adding *"to the whole Number of free Persons, including those bound to Service for a Term of Years, and excluding Indians not taxed, three fifths of all other Persons."* The term "free persons" referred to white men and women of any social class, including those known as "indentured servants" or "those bound to Service for a Term of Years." However, Native Americans, referred to as "Indians," were not counted for state populations. Slaves were included in the count, but only as three-fifths of a person, rather than each person being counted as one. This provision, known as the Three-Fifths Compromise, reflected the agreement among convention delegates that slaves would be considered as some form of a person but would count less than "free persons." While the terminology intentionally denoted slaves, the words "slave" or "slavery" were not directly used in the Constitution, although there were indirect references to the practice.

Delegates from northern states, where slavery was less prevalent, argued that slaves should not be counted for representation.

They believed that if southern states were allowed to include slaves in their population count, they would have a disproportionate share of representatives, even though slaves had no citizenship rights and could not contribute to the selection of elected representatives or any form of government. On the other hand, southern states advocated for a broader interpretation of representation and wanted slaves to count in order to increase their federal representation. The Three-Fifths Compromise, where slaves were counted as less than free persons, remained the method for distributing federal seats in Congress, which is also tied to the size of the Electoral College, until the Thirteenth Amendment was adopted in 1865, officially outlawing slavery.

During the founding period, there were 65 representatives, and over time, this number has increased through federal legislation to accommodate a greater number of representatives. Currently, there are 100 senators and 435 representatives, as specified in the Permanent Apportionment Act of 1929. There are also six nonvoting delegates from DC and the U.S. territories.[3] The members elected to the House have the responsibility of selecting their own Speaker of the House, and both the House and Senate determine their internal leadership structure. The vice president has the power to preside over the Senate, but only casts a vote in the event of a tie.

While serving as members of Congress in the House or Senate, legislators are prohibited from holding any other government jobs. This is why you often see members of Congress resign when a new president takes office and wants to appoint them as a chief of staff or leader of a federal agency.

According to the Constitution, legislators receive compensation set by federal law, which means they pass laws to determine their own salaries—more on this when we get to the Twenty-seventh Amendment. Currently, senators and representatives earn $174,000 per year, with additional compensation of $20,000 to $50,000 for leadership positions, and there is an annual cap of $31,815—in 2023—on the amount of additional, outside earnings a member of Congress can make. No federal officeholder can accept any present, emolument, office, or title from a foreign state or royalty without an individual exception granted by Congress.

Both representatives and senators must be residents of the state they seek to represent. In the House, members must be at least 25 years old and citizens for at least 7 years before taking office. Senators must be 30 years old and citizens for 9 years.

The House is led by the Speaker of the House, who is elected by the other members of House at the beginning of each Congress, and most often belongs to whichever party holds a majority in the chamber—though this is not a requirement. The Speaker, who holds the third position in the line of presidential succession, has many responsibilities: being the point person for media interviews, determining which members are appointed to different congressional committees, and, most importantly, deciding which pieces of legislation will be considered with the House Rules Committee—an important power called *gatekeeping*.

You've probably heard of two of the most recent speakers. California's Nancy Pelosi served as Speaker, first from 2007 to 2011 as the first woman to ever hold the position and again from 2019 to 2023, representing the Democratic party. Kevin McCarthy, also from California, was a notable speaker from the Republican party who was ousted in October 2023 after eight fellow Republicans decided to pass a motion to replace him. All House Democrats joined in that effort and then House Republicans had to squabble for three full weeks to nominate and vote for his replacement, Speaker Mike Johnson from Louisiana.

Speakers are also called *party leaders*, and when voting for a speaker, members of the parties in Congress also vote for other positions to form a leadership team of legislators who are elevated to help the speaker do their job. These other leadership jobs are not mentioned in the Constitution, but are a norm that Congress keeps in place to delegate leadership tasks to multiple people. Other positions include the majority leader from the party that controls more seats, the party whip who is responsible for knowing who will and won't vote for specific pieces of legislation, the minority leader from the minority party or parties in Congress, and others that a specific Speaker may wish to create.

In the Senate, the vice president of the United States serves as the "President of the Senate" and can cast the tie-breaking vote if needed. However, the scheduling of bills is typically decided cooperatively by the majority and minority leaders, who are selected by members of the Senate. Majority and minority leaders act as the spokespeople for their parties, and the majority leader is the senatorial counterpart to the Speaker of the House—though the Constitution does not outline broad duties for this position. There is a more ceremonial position in the Senate known as the *president pro tempore*—and this person is the fourth in line for presidential succession.

Every state is afforded two senators and at least one representative. The number of representatives is tied to population, giving larger states a larger delegation in the House. Each state, no matter how small, is guaranteed at least one representative. Currently, the ratio is approximately 757,000 people per representative. This means that all states with fewer than 1.12 million people have the same number of representatives in Congress. For example, our least populous state, Wyoming, with an estimated population of 579,495 people according to the 2020 Census, has the same number of representatives as Montana, which has a population of 1,103,187.

The House and Senate have a few specific responsibilities, with the Senate mattering more for foreign policy and executive appointments, while the House holds special legislative powers.

Both have powers related to impeachment, though here too, they have specific roles. The Senate confirms presidential appointments for executive and judicial nominees. Additionally, treaties with other nations must be approved by a two-thirds vote in the Senate. All bills related to taxation or government revenues must originate in the House of Representatives. The founders designed the House as the chamber representing the people, believing that its members, being more closely connected to their constituents than senators with statewide constituencies, should be responsible for issues concerning government funding and public support.

The House is tasked with initiating impeachment proceedings against executive or judicial branch officials, with the Senate conducting the impeachment proceedings. To remove someone from their position through impeachment, a two-thirds majority in the Senate must agree. While presidential impeachment has become increasingly politically motivated, it is highly unlikely that an impeachment effort will succeed in removing a president unless a large majority of the Congress is from a different party than the president. While impeachment of a president is rare, federal judges have been more frequently impeached and removed, totaling 15 to date. Impeachment only leads to removal from office and disqualification from future federal positions, without additional civil or criminal consequences.

The legislative branch's primary power is to make laws. In making the laws, legislators essentially devise and update the rules of the game. The Constitution remains the supreme law of the land, but Congress can pass laws they want to and until those laws are challenged in court or repealed, they remain enforceable. Congress also engages in oversight, investigation, and budget distribution. Central to Congress's duties is the "power of the purse," which allows it to raise taxes and fund government initiatives.

The Constitution requires both the House and Senate to pass identical versions of a bill, which then needs the president's signature to become law. Over time, Congress has developed detailed procedures, largely managed by specialized committees, to efficiently handle the passage of hundreds of laws each year. Though these procedures are not outlined in the Constitution, I briefly outline them here.

The committee system in Congress, established in 1946 by the Legislative Reorganization Act, is where legislative work occurs. Committees oversee government agencies and sectors, debate and amend bills, and can summon experts for testimony. Committee chairs act as gatekeepers for legislation within their domain.

Members of Congress are assigned to various committees by the Speaker of the House based on their stated preferences. The majority versus minority split of each individual committee reflects the split of Congress as a whole; for example, when there is a Congress made of 60% Democrats and 40% Republicans, each of the committees is made up of roughly 60% Democrats and 40% Republicans. Committee leadership is often decided by seniority. Types of committees include standing committees on ongoing issues like appropriations, rules, and foreign affairs; subcommittees for specific areas within a larger committee (i.e. the subcommittee on Middle East, North Africa, and Global Counterterrorism) sits within the standing House Foreign Affairs Committee; select committees for special inquiries; joint committees with members from both the House and Senate; and the Committee of the Whole, involving all House members. While the Senate also organizes work through committees, the process differs due to its smaller size—individual members tend to matter more in a body of 100 than a body of 441.

Legislation begins with drafting, where legislators, often with input from interest groups, write a bill. It's formally introduced to Congress by a member, known as the sponsor, with supporters joining as co-sponsors. The number of co-sponsors can be a good indicator of a bill's potential success.

Leadership then assigns the bill to the relevant committee(s), with some bills undergoing *multiple referrals* to various committees, potentially slowing their progress. In committee, a smaller subcommittee may further scrutinize the bill, including conducting hearings and seeking expert opinions, such as financial impact assessments from the Congressional Budget Office. Committees refine bills through amendments or complete overhauls during markup sessions. A majority vote within the committee then decides if a bill proceeds to the full chamber. Without majority support, bills often stall, unless a discharge petition—requiring a majority from the entire chamber—resurrects them for a full vote. Most legislation doesn't advance beyond committee; in the 116th Congress, only 9.6% of bills reached full House consideration.

Leadership conducts vote whipping to secure the necessary support for a bill's passage before it's presented for a chamber-wide vote. Both the House and Senate have legislators who are elected to serve as *whips*, who are the people responsible for securing party support on legislation and counting potential votes. They use political strategies to sway legislators, often through promises of campaign assistance or other political favors. Though their work is behind the scenes, the role of a whip is an important rung for climbing the political ladder. Votes typically proceed only if passage is likely or if there's strategic value, even in likely defeat. For instance, House Republicans repeatedly voted to repeal Obamacare (the Affordable Care Act) during 2010–2012, not expecting success but to fulfill campaign promises.

Roll call votes in Congress record each member's decision, but many decisions are made by voice vote, where members shout "yea" or "no," and the presiding officer determines the result without recording individual votes. The Senate sometimes uses *unanimous consent* to expedite voting by setting aside formal rules. Very few bills make it through Congress; in the 116th Congress, only 8.9% passed one chamber, and only 1.9% passed both. Ultimately, just 344 bills or 1.6% of introduced bills were enacted into law, either by presidential signature or by overriding a veto.

The president's most significant legislative power is the *veto*, a "no" that can stop legislation approved by Congress. Once Congress passes a bill, the president has 10 days to sign it into law. If the president vetoes a bill, it returns to Congress with their objections. Congress can override this veto with a two-thirds majority in both chambers. The president can also execute a "pocket veto" by not signing a bill when Congress adjourns within the 10-day period, which cannot be overridden. To avoid a pocket veto, Congress refrains from adjourning if they suspect the president might not sign a bill they wish to pass. If the president doesn't sign a bill but Congress remains in session for 10 days after passage, the bill becomes law without the president's signature.

The Constitution mandates the president to veto a bill in its entirety, not just parts of it. President Clinton briefly exercised a line-item veto to reject specific portions of bills, but the Supreme Court struck down this power and interpreted Article I to mean that he must consider full bills, otherwise he would be trampling on the legislative power of Congress by being able to make modifications.[4] While a president cannot officially veto parts of a bill, they can use the threat of a veto to influence Congress to amend a bill before it reaches their desk.

The Constitution originally placed specific restrictions on Congressional legislation, particularly around the importation of individuals, which was a veiled reference to the slave trade. It forbade any laws altering this trade before 1808, reflecting the contentious debate over slavery during the nation's founding.

Beyond legislating, Congress has additional powers. It can raise government revenues through federal income taxes, fees, and duties on imported goods. Congress also holds the ability to coin money and regulate commerce within the United States. It is responsible for authorizing and appropriating funds for different programs. Its constitutional powers extend to military oversight, including the declaration of war and military funding. Furthermore, Congress is the sole governing body capable of defining and punishing "Piracies and Felonies committed on the high Seas," and Congress has specific powers to govern Washington DC.

This article also establishes the federal form of government, with certain powers reserved for the federal government and others for states. To ensure smooth operations across state lines, the Constitution prohibits states from imposing duties on goods imported or exported by residents of other states. States are prohibited from conducting independent foreign policy, minting their own currencies, granting noble titles, imposing duties on imported goods, or entering agreements with foreign powers to house troops or engage in military activities. While many founders aimed to protect robust states' rights, these provisions corrected the shortcomings of the Articles of Confederation, ensuring a unified federal approach while safeguarding state rights.

Five Things to Know About Article 1

Structure of Congress: Article 1 establishes Congress as the federal legislative branch, consisting of two chambers—the House of Representatives and the Senate. Representatives are elected every two years, while senators are elected for six-year terms.

Enumerated Powers: Article 1 outlines the specific powers granted to Congress, known as the enumerated powers. These include the authority to levy taxes, regulate interstate and foreign commerce, coin money, establish post offices, declare war, and maintain the armed forces. The enumerated powers provide Congress with a wide range of responsibilities and authority.

Legislative Process: Article 1 details the legislative process, requiring both the House and the Senate to pass identical versions of a bill before it can become law. This process involves committee reviews, debates, and voting in both chambers. Additionally, the president's signature is required for a bill to become fully enforceable law.

Limitations on States: Article 1 specifies that states are prohibited from imposing certain duties, conducting independent foreign policy, minting currencies, or entering agreements with foreign powers without congressional approval.

Impeachment and Removal: Article 1 grants Congress the authority to impeach and remove federal officials, including the president, vice president, and judges. Impeachment is initiated by the House of Representatives, and if the accused is found guilty by the Senate with a two-thirds majority, they can be removed from office.

Article 2 – The Executive Branch

The Constitution was very different from the Articles of Confederation—in part because the Constitution gave power to a single executive—the president. During the Constitutional Convention, the framers worked to balance the fear of authoritarian rule against the need for decisive leadership; group work is hard at the top. They modeled the presidency on state governors, ensuring a central figure to enforce congressional laws while guarding against tyranny.

The president enforces laws passed by Congress, leads the executive branch, and, with the vice president, represents U.S. interests at home and abroad. That is a lot of power for one person.

To qualify for the presidency, someone has to be a natural-born U.S. citizen, have resided in the United States for 14 years, and be at least 35 years old—the highest age requirement for elected federal office. The president's current $400,000 annual salary, set by Congress, remains fixed throughout their term. While Congress can adjust the salary for future presidents, it cannot change the sitting president's pay as a punitive or favorable measure. The first president, George Washington was paid $25,000 a year—which was about 2% of the federal budget. If that were the presidential salary today, it would be about $851,000 based on the dollar amount or $122,600,000,000 if it were based on 2% of the total federal budget.

The president has the power to summon Congress for the State of the Union Address, usually given each January. This address is a chance for the president to outline their agenda and report on the nation's condition, though the Constitution doesn't mandate its frequency or specifics.

The president has many powers, including acting as Commander in Chief of the armed forces, seeking updates from executive officials, granting pardons, and appointing federal judges, ambassadors, and agency heads with Senate approval.[5] The Constitution says very little about the executive branch's departments but acknowledges their existence and grants Congress the authority to establish additional departments if necessary. Initially, four departments were established: Treasury, State, War, and Justice. Now there are 15, with the most recently added Homeland Security established in 2002 after the 9/11 attacks. When you hear about the president's *cabinet*, that is a reference to the people who lead those agencies and a few other positions within the executive branch.

The only legal method to remove a president outlined in the original Constitution is through impeachment. Impeachment charges can include "Treason, Bribery, or other high Crimes and Misdemeanors," which is a broad and flexible concept. In 1967, the Twenty-fifth Amendment was adopted, which permits legal removal of the president through an effort of the vice president and a majority of the cabinet with final decision-making left to the Congress.

The Electoral College

The Electoral College, a uniquely American institution outlined in Article 2 of the Constitution, differs from other U.S. elections where the popular vote determines the winner. Instead, the Electoral College, only used in presidential and vice presidential elections, winners are determined by a majority of state *electors* with each state having a number of electors equal to their congressional representation (representatives and senators). Although voters see presidential candidates' names on their ballot, they technically vote for pledged electors.

The smallest states have at least 3 electors, while the largest, California, had 55 in 2020. Washington DC also has 3 electors, per the Twenty-third Amendment. The number of electors for each state changes based on the reapportionment of House seats after each Census. The process of tabulating and allocating voters' votes into Electoral College votes differs from any other election in the United States. Let's look at Pennsylvania to see how the Electoral College process differs from standard popular elections.

Pennsylvania has 20 electors and approximately 6.8 million people voted in the 2020 election. Only 80,555 more voters chose Joe Biden over Donald Trump. However, due to the winner-take-all system of the Electoral College, all 20 electors from Pennsylvania counted for Joe Biden, rather than a potential split of 11–9 or 10–10 if a different allocation system were used. In that same election, nine House seats were won by Democrats and nine by Republicans in Pennsylvania, reflecting the political differences of its people. However, in the Electoral College, all 20 state votes went to Joe Biden. Except for Nebraska and Maine, all other states use this winner-take-all style of aggregation, making strategically important states with high numbers of electors and politically divided populations pivotal for presidential campaigns.

To win a majority in the Electoral College, a candidate needs at least 270 out of the total 538 Electoral College votes. This is the total of the sum of 100 senators, 435 representatives, and three electors from Washington DC—which is the math spelled out in the Constitution.

The vice president, serving as the president of the Senate, officially tallies the Electoral College votes—which in practice means receiving and certifying the vote tallies done at the state level. If no presidential candidate wins the required 270 majority or if there's an electoral tie, the House of Representatives chooses the president. In that scenario, each state delegation casts one vote among the top five candidates. This method decided the 1800 and 1824 elections.

Initially, the Electoral College elected the president, with the runner-up becoming vice president. One only needs to imagine how a President Donald Trump and Vice President Hillary Clinton would have worked together to understand how much of an error this original idea was. Soon after ratification of the Constitution, the Twelfth Amendment modified this part of the article, separating the votes for each office to ensure cohesive leadership. Both the president and the vice president serve four-year terms.

Five Things to Know About Article 2

Presidential Requirements: The president must be a natural-born citizen, at least 35 years old, and have lived in the United States for 14 years.

Presidential Powers: The president is the head of the executive branch, with powers such as being the Commander in Chief, appointing officials with Senate approval, granting pardons, and making treaties.

State of the Union Address: The president can convene Congress to deliver the State of the Union Address, typically held in January, to discuss the administration's plans and the nation's status.

Impeachment: Impeachment is the only legal method outlined in Article 2 to remove a president and requires charges of "Treason, Bribery, or other high Crimes and Misdemeanors."

Executive Departments: The Constitution mentions the existence of executive departments, and Congress can establish more.

Article 3 – The Judiciary

The Constitution gives minimal details about the judicial branch, specifying only that the judicial power resides in the Supreme Court and other lower courts established by Congress. It spells out that judges hold their positions for life, subject to good behavior, and cannot have their salaries altered during their terms. The Constitution does not stipulate judges' age, citizenship, or number, leaving Congress to define these. The Supreme Court serves as the final appellate court, with most cases progressing through district and circuit courts first, except those under the Supreme Court's original jurisdiction. The Supreme Court's original jurisdiction includes cases involving federal officials, international matters, maritime law, state disputes, and territorial issues.

Read in conjunction with the first 10 amendments, the Constitutions states that federal criminal trials require a jury in the state where the crime was committed, and civil trials also have the right to a jury.

In Article 3, treason is defined as waging war against the United States or aiding its enemies, with conviction requiring two witnesses or a confession. It notes that Congress has the power to set treason penalties, but that those penalties must only apply to the convicted individual—and not be extended to members of their family or friends not convicted of such a crime.

Five Things to Know About Article 3

Judicial Power: Article 3 establishes one Supreme Court and other lower courts appointed by Congress.

Judicial Terms: Judges serve for life unless impeached.

> *Supreme Court Original Jurisdiction:* It handles cases involving federal appointees, foreign powers, high seas issues, disputes between states, and territorial disputes.
>
> *Criminal Trials:* Federal criminal trials require a jury and must be held in the state where the crime occurred.
>
> *Treason:* Treason includes levying war against the United States or aiding enemies. Conviction requires two witnesses or an open confession.

Article 4 – The States

Article 4 of the Constitution ensures the integrity of state actions, records, and judicial proceedings across state lines. It mandates that each state must recognize the official acts and legal decisions of every other state—for instance, a marriage license from one state is valid in all others—this is known as the *full faith and credit clause*.

This article also establishes *citizens*' rights, differing from earlier sections that referred to persons more generally. It grants citizens of each state the same *privileges and immunities* as citizens of any other state they visit or move to. This language delineates the status of citizenship, implying that not all residents are granted equal status under the law.

Article 4 mandates the return of any person charged with a crime who flees to another state back to the state where the offense occurred. Originally, this also included an implicit reference to escaped slaves, stating those "held to Service or Labour" must be returned to their original state upon escape. This clause, addressing slavery indirectly, became obsolete with the Thirteenth Amendment's prohibition of slavery.

The article sets out the process for admitting new states, prohibiting the creation of, or merging of states without the consent of the involved state legislatures and Congress. Congress also has the authority to manage U.S. territories. Furthermore, it requires states to maintain a republican form of government, ensuring power lies with the people and their representatives, and underscores the states' duty to protect citizens' rights and welfare.

Five Things to Know About Article 4

Full Faith and Credit: States must recognize and honor legal acts and records from other states.

Privileges and Immunities: Citizens have the same rights when traveling to another state.

Extradition and Slavery: Fugitives charged with crimes must be returned to the state where the offense was committed. The article also obliquely references slavery, requiring the return of escaped slaves to their owners.

Formation of New States: New states can't be carved out of existing ones or merge without consent from state legislatures and Congress.

Republican Form of Government: States must have a government where power comes from the people.

Article 5 – Amendments

Article 5 of the U.S. Constitution lays out two methods of proposing amendments to the Constitution. An amendment can be proposed by either a two-thirds majority vote in both the House and Senate or by a convention called for by two-thirds of state legislatures. Ratification requires the approval of three-fourths of the states, currently 38 out of 50. To date, all of our amendments have originated in Congress rather than constitutional conventions. Because it's unclear how a convention would work or what limits would be in place—not to mention how hard it would be to have so many states coordinate and agree to do something—it's likely that any future amendments would probably also start within the Congress. Our most recent amendment was adopted in 1992, but really the 1970s was the last time Congress got to working on proposing amendments in a realistic way. We'll talk more about this when we get to the amendments.

Article 5 of the Constitution originally protected the slave trade from any sort of change or amendment before 1808, saying, "No Amendment which may be made prior to the Year One thousand eight hundred and eight shall in any Manner affect the first and fourth Clauses in the Ninth Section of the first Article." It also ensured that no state can be denied equal numbers of Senators in the Senate without its consent.

There aren't really five things you need to know about Article 5, but here are three takeaways.

Three Things to Know About Article 5

Amendment Process: Amendments can be proposed if two-thirds of both the House and the Senate agree, or if two-thirds of the state legislatures call a convention for proposing amendments.

Ratification: To ratify an amendment, three-fourths of the states must agree through either a state legislature vote or a state convention.

Safeguards: Article 5 ensures that no state can be denied equal suffrage in the Senate without its consent, guaranteeing each state an equal number of senators.

Article 6 – Debts, Supremacy, Oaths

Article 6 addresses national debt and affirms the Constitution's supremacy, necessitating clear federal financial controls post–Revolutionary War due to states' unequal debts and inadequate tax revenue sharing under the Articles of Confederation.

The article states that the federal government assumes state debts accrued prior to the Constitution's adoption. It establishes the Constitution as the supreme law that all states and judges must abide by. Additionally, it declares that government officials must take a personal oath to support the Constitution, but no religious test can be administered for public office. The inclusion of this provision was necessary as religious diversity, tolerance, and recognition of nonreligious individuals were vital political priorities during the time of increasing state populations, immigration, and westward expansion.

Three Things to Know About Article 6

National Debt: The article acknowledges the federal government's assumption of state debts accumulated before the Constitution's adoption.

Supremacy Clause: Article 6 establishes the Constitution as the supreme law of the land.

No Religious Test: The article prohibits religious tests as requirements for holding public office. Government officials are required to take a personal oath to support the Constitution but cannot be subjected to religious discrimination.

Article 7 – Ratification

The final article of the Constitution is a simple sentence: "The Ratification of the Conventions of nine States shall be sufficient for the Establishment of this Constitution between the States so ratifying the Same."

On September 17, 1787, the delegates at the convention concluded their work and signed the proposed U.S. Constitution. To bring the Constitution into effect and replace the Articles of Confederation, at least 9 out of the 13 states had to ratify it.

Delaware became the first state to ratify on December 7, 1787. Shortly after, Pennsylvania, New Jersey, Georgia, and Connecticut did as well. However, some states hesitated because the Constitution didn't explicitly outline the rights of citizens. In Massachusetts, opponents of ratification were convinced to support it on the condition that a set of citizen rights would be proposed once the new Constitution was agreed upon. This agreement, known as the Massachusetts Compromise, led to both the Bill of Rights and ratification by Massachusetts, Maryland, South Carolina, and New Hampshire. As a result, the Constitution came into effect on March 9, 1789.

The Bill of Rights

Kids may find themselves particularly excited once they get into learning about the amendments to the Constitution, with a special focus on the Bill of Rights—which are the first 10 amendments to the Constitution. While the Constitution itself may seem distant, the amendments are easier to connect to our everyday lives. From freedom of speech and religion to the right to fair treatment, exploring the amendments and the Bill of Rights can inspire kids to know about their own rights and defend those of others.

The Bill of Rights serves as a first set of individual rights in America. Its principles have been widely celebrated, referenced, and explored in various forms of media. *The Fifth Estate* (2013) about the creators of Wikileaks is about the First Amendment. *Bowling for Columbine* (2002) takes on the Second Amendment. The Fifth and Sixth Amendments are frequently invoked in courtroom dramas, where characters reference the freedom from self-incrimination, and the right to a fair trial. This is to say that the stories that can be told using the amendments are powerful and you can turn to other media to keep talking about a specific issue.

Before, during, and after ratification of the Constitution, there were calls for the adoption of amendments to provide explicit rights for the people. Recall that the Constitution simply describes the government, but says nearly nothing about the positive rights that people enjoy, other than:

- To be counted for representation.
- For citizens to have the right to vote for their representatives in the House and for presidents through the Electoral College.
- To be provided with a jury trial in criminal cases.
- To have legal actions in one state be honored in another state.
- To be free from religious tests when seeking public office.

Beyond those few promises—the rights of people and citizens in the new federal entity were quite cloudy. In this section, I'll give you a breakdown of the amendments, how they work, and a set of conversation starter ideas that you can use with your kids. Your kids will also probably have questions not covered here, and for that you can practice doing joint research with them. If you simply go online and type in any amendment, you'll be able to find loads of questions, debating ideas, and contexts to consider—we are awash in this sort of content and information. Treat the following section as your introduction to the amendments and how to talk about them, and know that if and when you need more to talk about things with your kids, it will be very easy to get that information.

First Amendment

Congress shall make no law respecting an establishment of religion, or prohibiting the free exercise thereof; or abridging the freedom of speech, or of the press; or the right of the people peaceably to assemble, and to petition the Government for a redress of grievances.

The First Amendment says that Congress cannot establish a national religion or restrict religious freedom of the people. It also provides for the freedom of speech, press, assembly, and the right to petition the government. These protections reflected the framers concern about how the Church of England tried to influence government *and* their wish to support religious diversity in the new nation full of immigrants holding many different religious and nonreligious outlooks.

The First Amendment upholds our freedom to express ideas, even unpopular ones. But when discussing it with your kids, it's important to note that this freedom has boundaries; it doesn't cover perjury, false claims, harmful rumors, hate speech, or speech that incites violence. Discussing the limits can help them grasp the government's role in balancing free expression with maintaining order and safety—which is a good way to start thinking about how much of our governing is done in shades of gray, rather than in an absolutist, black-or-white understanding of the law.

Children may have questions about the overlap of religion and government, such as hearing "one nation Under God" when reciting the Pledge or seeing "In God We Trust" on money. Researching together the historical politics of World War II and the Cold War can shed light on why these instances are not considered a violation of the First Amendment. It will also help children grasp that many aspects of our actions operate in an interpretative zone rather than definitive right or wrong.

When discussing association, peaceable assembly, and petition, you can talk to your kids about protest movements you may have participated in and ask them about causes they might want to protest about someday. If you have children who want to consider the amendment, you can provide them with some conversation starter questions and ask them to come up with arguments for each side:

- Should insulting speech that falls short of hate rhetoric be protected?

- Are there any sorts of expression that the government should have a right to prohibit? What about around areas of national security?

- Are there any instances in which the government should ban the press from covering certain stories?

- What are the limits to what's considered "speech"? Is art speech? Is money speech? Is computer coding speech?

Second Amendment

A well regulated Militia, being necessary to the security of a free State, the right of the people to keep and bear Arms, shall not be infringed.

The Second Amendment is a source of ongoing controversy, both during its drafting and in present times, albeit for different reasons. When the amendment was being written, the framers took into account existing state laws, which influenced its wording. However, the specific phrasing of the amendment has led to disputes and varying interpretations since its adoption.

During the Revolutionary era, established towns would often engage in mustering drills where boys and men who were capable and could afford arms would gather to practice how to protect their communities.[6] These groups were sometimes referred to as militias. Town militias were more commonplace because the founders and people of that time were cautious about a standing army controlled by the government due to their experiences with standing armies under the British Crown—which were occasionally used against the people.[7]

The debate on gun control versus gun rights is a major point of contention in American politics.

Regardless of your stance on guns—as owners, users, proponents of stricter laws, or having no affiliation—it's important to consider the perspectives of those who hold different views. Despite the Second Amendment at the federal level, gun laws and ownership regulations differ significantly across the United States, with most states striving to find the right balance that serves their populations.

Conversations with children about guns may inevitably lead to discussing violent incidents, such as school or public area shootings. These concerns are relevant when considering the amendment, and you should be open to having honest conversations with your kids. To help them understand why this amendment was included in our Constitution, it's helpful to reflect on how the world was different in 1791 compared to today. You can prompt your children to think about these differences by asking questions such as:

- What does the word militia mean to you, have you heard it before?

- How might gun ownership in 1791 be different than gun ownership today?

- Can you imagine what it would take to overthrow a government as a new people?

- Do you think it would be possible to live in a country where individuals don't own firearms?

- Do you think it's still relevant in today's society, considering the differences between the world in 1791 and the world we live in now?

Third Amendment

No Soldier shall, in time of peace be quartered in any house, without the consent of the Owner, nor in time of war, but in a manner to be prescribed by law.

The Third Amendment may not have much impact on today's politics, but it held significance when it was adopted. During the Revolutionary War and other military conflicts, soldiers and armies would sometimes take over the homes of private individuals, seeking shelter and preparing for war—even if private homeowners did not wish to give up their land and property. Understandably, this deeply troubled the home-owners, leading to the inclusion of this amendment in our Constitution.

While it's highly unlikely that such controversies will arise today, you can still ask your children to consider what it would be like if they had to give up their rooms or even their entire house for the military. Encourage them to think about the con-cept of personal space and the importance of protecting one's home, even in times of war or conflict. Here are some questions to start those conversations:

- Have you ever heard of soldiers or military personnel stay-ing in people's homes during times of war or conflict? How do you think that would feel?

- Why do you think the founders of the United States felt it was important to include the Third Amendment in the Bill of Rights?

- Can you think of any situations in modern times where the Third Amendment could still be relevant or applicable?

Fourth Amendment

The right of the people to be secure in their persons, houses, papers, and effects, against unreasonable searches and seizures, shall not be violated, and no Warrants shall issue, but upon prob-able cause, supported by Oath or affirmation, and particularly describing the place to be searched, and the persons or things to be seized.

The Fourth Amendment grants people the right to be "secure in their persons, houses, papers, and effects, against unreasonable searches and seizures." This means that any warrants calling for the search and potential seizure of property must be based on probable cause, clearly defined in scope, and authorized by a judge or other legitimate government representative responsible for this task.

When discussing this amendment with school-aged children, they might relate to the idea of protecting their things from the oversight of parents or school administrators. The notion of having privacy in their own room or locker resonates with most kids as they grow up and increasingly seek their own independence. On this note, you can point out that federal amendments do not dictate how you enforce household rules, and there are exceptions and specific rules for how schools address privacy concerns.

When discussing this topic with your children, it might be helpful to focus on the context of school searches versus police searches, as it allows them to better grasp their rights. Despite that fact, school and home "search and seizure" rules are not subject to limitations under the Fourth Amendment. Talking about the significance of this amendment from unwarranted government intrusion will probably be of interest to older teens. Those who have cars or are looking to live on their own will have an easier time understanding the fair or unfair application of law in light of the Fourth Amendment.

- Are there any instances in which it would be okay for your school to search your locker without your permission?

- Does it matter if you are enrolled in a public or private school when considering the protections of the Fourth Amendment for items in your locker?

- Should minors be protected in the same way adults are? Why or why not?

- If the school monitored all the texts sent over its internet during school hours, would that be a violation of the Fourth Amendment?

- Is there ever a time police should be allowed to search an area without first obtaining a warrant?

Fifth Amendment

No person shall be held to answer for a capital, or otherwise infamous crime, unless on a presentment or indictment of a Grand Jury, except in cases arising in the land or naval forces, or in the Militia, when in actual service in time of War or public danger; nor shall any person be subject for the same offence to be twice put in jeopardy of life or limb; nor shall be compelled in any criminal case to be a witness against himself, nor be deprived of life, liberty, or property, without due process of law; nor shall private property be taken for public use, without just compensation.

The Fifth Amendment, the longest among the Bill of Rights, encompasses several important protections. First, it grants citizens some input and control over government prosecutions. A person cannot be charged with a crime unless a grand jury, composed of citizens, determines that the government has sufficient evidence to proceed.[8] Second, the amendment safeguards against double jeopardy, ensuring that no person can be tried for the same offense twice. Third, the famous phrase "I plead the Fifth" refers to the protection against self-incrimination, where a person cannot be compelled to testify against themselves in criminal cases. Fourth, the amendment establishes that individuals cannot be deprived of life, liberty, or property without due process of law. And finally, it introduces the concept of eminent domain, allowing the government to take private property for public use, but with the condition that just compensation must be provided.

For most kids, these protections, along with the other rights of the accused, may seem abstract and challenging to grasp in relation to their own lives. When initiating a conversation with your kids, it's not necessary for them to fully understand these protections. Instead, focus on conveying the limitations imposed by our form of government. You are laying the groundwork for them to gradually understand the topic and to be able to grasp more and more as they get older.

Highlighting the role of the grand jury is particularly important, as it is one of the few ways individual citizens can influence the decisions made by government prosecutors. It's also one of the things my college students are least likely to be aware of. In criminal proceedings, prosecutors must convince the grand jury of the worthiness of their case before going to trial. Essentially, they are asking for consent from citizens to use government resources in pursuing legal action against an alleged criminal. Giving that power to the people is quite a good check on the government. As young people near voting age and potential jury service, going through how that service effects the government and individual lives will allow them to better understand their role and responsibilities.

You can talk to your kids about what it means when someone "pleads the Fifth" or refuses to answer questions that could potentially incriminate themselves. Is it an admission of guilt or simply the exercise of a fundamental right? It's worth noting that these Fifth Amendment protections only apply to criminal charges.

So, while your kids may try to plead the Fifth when you ask them about their whereabouts after curfew or their role in why their sibling is crying, they still have to answer questions about their actions as these are not criminal matters.

When talking about what we mean by the "due process of law," you can emphasize the importance of fairness and the idea that individuals in the United States are presumed innocent until proven guilty in criminal trials.

The concept of eminent domain allows for public needs to sometimes override private property rights. Discuss with your children how this principle has been applied in your local area, perhaps in the creation of roads, public buildings, or utilities. Investigating local instances of eminent domain provides a practical view of the Fifth Amendment and offers a window into your community's political decision-making processes. Here are few questions to get into this topic:

- Why do you think someone might choose not to answer certain questions in a legal situation?

- What does it mean to be presumed innocent until proven guilty in a criminal trial?

- Can you think of any situations where you might feel torn between your right to protect yourself from self-incrimination and the expectation to provide information?

- Have you ever wondered why the government sometimes takes private property for public use? How do you think the Fifth Amendment's requirement of fair compensation for property owners helps maintain a balance between individual rights and community needs?

- Do you know of any examples in our community where the government has used eminent domain?

Sixth Amendment

In all criminal prosecutions, the accused shall enjoy the right to a speedy and public trial, by an impartial jury of the State and district wherein the crime shall have been committed, which district shall have been previously ascertained by law, and to be informed of the nature and cause of the accusation; to be confronted with the witnesses against him; to have compulsory process for obtaining witnesses in his favor, and to have the Assistance of Counsel for his defence.

This amendment ensures that in criminal cases—where the government accuses individuals of crimes with potential punishments—accused persons have the right to:

- Speedy and public trials.
- Impartial juries.
- Be informed of the charges against them.
- Learn about the prosecution's witnesses.
- Summon witnesses in their favor to support their case.
- Have legal counsel for their defense.

When discussing this amendment with your children, talk about the idea of fairness in government actions and the reasons for being concerned about being falsely accused of a crime. If a government didn't have to inform individuals why they were being held or what charges they were facing, it would have almost unlimited power to detain people without accountability. Without public trials with citizen juries, people could be easily imprisoned without any public outcry or intervention. The guarantee of legal counsel (a lawyer) ensures that everyone, regardless of their financial means, can be represented in trials by someone who knows the law. Although these rights specifically apply to individuals accused of crimes, the underlying principles protect all of us and are worth considering with your kids.

- What do you think could happen if this right didn't exist?
- Do you think it's important for criminal defendants to have access to the witnesses used for the prosecution?
- What do you think it means to have an impartial jury?
- Imagine you were accused of a crime. Why do you think the right to bring witnesses is important?
- Do you think everyone should have the right to legal counsel in criminal proceedings?

Seventh Amendment

In Suits at common law, where the value in controversy shall exceed twenty dollars, the right of trial by jury shall be preserved, and no fact tried by a jury, shall be otherwise reexamined in any Court of the United States, than according to the rules of the common law.

The Seventh Amendment extends the right to a jury trial to those involved in civil suits where the value of the claim exceeds $20. Although this amount hasn't changed since 1791, it would be equivalent to about $664.54 in 2024.

The Sixth and Seventh Amendments serve as a teaching points about the distinctions between criminal and civil cases. In criminal trials, the government prosecutes, potentially resulting in punishment like imprisonment. Civil cases involve disputes between individuals or entities, focusing on restitution or compensation. Criminal convictions require proof beyond a reasonable doubt, a higher standard than civil cases, which are based on the preponderance of the evidence. With your older children you can think about what it costs to actually start a lawsuit and begin a discussion about why things sometimes happen that aren't technically "legal" but do not rise to the level of a lawsuit because of effort involved in navigating the legal system. Here are two questions you might ask on this subject:

- Do you know the difference between a criminal case and a civil case?

- Would you prefer to have a jury decide the outcome or have a judge make the decision if you were in a trial?

Eighth Amendment

Excessive bail shall not be required, nor excessive fines imposed, nor cruel and unusual punishments inflicted.

The Eighth Amendment says that bail should be set at a reasonable amount based on an accused person's means, and if someone is found guilty of a crime, only punishments that are not considered cruel or unusual should be applied.

What constitutes "cruel and unusual" varies, and our standards have changed over time. Some punishments that were once accepted may now be seen as cruel or inhumane. When discussing this with teenagers, it's okay to explore the historical punishments we used to allow but no longer do. Standards around torture have changed, as have the severity of punishments relative to the crimes committed. While the death penalty, also known as capital punishment, has been deemed constitutional, the Supreme Court has ruled against executing individuals with intellectual disabilities or those who committed crimes while under the age of 18 as it violates the Eighth Amendment.

The provision regarding excessive bail can also open a discussion about economic justice. When a person is arrested, they are still presumed innocent until proven guilty. However, in many states and in the federal system, there are provisions for detaining accused people unless they can post bail. Posting bail means handing over a sum of money and agreeing to a set of conditions to allow someone accused of a crime to be released from custody until their court appearance. Final bail determinations are made considering the financial situation of the accused, ensuring that people from different economic backgrounds can leave custody while awaiting trial or the next steps in the legal proceedings. But like all politics, there is no bright line for what's too much or too little, and instead here, too, things operate in a gray zone. Here are three questions that will help you and your child think about this amendment:

- What does the phrase "cruel and unusual punishment" mean to you?

- Why do you think it's important for punishments to be fair and not too harsh?

- Do you think bail should be set based on a person's ability to pay? Why or why not?

Ninth Amendment

The enumeration in the Constitution, of certain rights, shall not be construed to deny or disparage others retained by the people.

The Ninth Amendment acknowledges the Constitution may not list all existing rights, but that other rights, though not specifically spelled out, might still be protected. A fun way to explore this topic with your kids is to ask them what other rights they would have included in the Constitution if they were part of the founding. Once they've come up with some ideas, you can try to find connections with existing rights and discuss how their proposed rights might already be covered—or might not be. Another way to lead this discussion is to ask why they think the certain rights they came up with don't exist at the Constitutional level. Encourage them to think about any potential unintended consequences if those rights were enjoyed and claimed by everyone. This amendment is an interesting one in that it does not provide for any one specific right, but rather a broader ability to claim rights that hadn't yet been specified. Here are conversation starter questions:

- Can you come up with an example of a right that is not specifically listed in the Constitution but is still important to you?

- Why do you think the Founding Fathers included the Ninth Amendment in the Constitution?

- If you could add a new right to the Constitution, what would it be and why?

Tenth Amendment

The powers not delegated to the United States by the Constitution, nor prohibited by it to the States, are reserved to the States respectively, or to the people.

The final inclusion in the Bill of Rights is an amendment that serves as a catch-all provision, protecting the roles of both states and the people. It reserves powers not granted to the federal government to the states or the people, addressing concerns that the new federal government could overpower states' authority. This is one that supports the idea that we—the people—are those who ultimately retain the powers of determining how our government ought to operate.

- Why do you think it was important for the founders to include the Tenth Amendment in the Bill of Rights?
- Can you think of any examples of powers or responsibilities that might belong to the states or the people according to the Tenth Amendment?

Beyond the Bill of Rights

Seventeen amendments have been added to the Constitution after the Bill of Rights, each addressing a significant national issue at the time of adoption. One way to stay engaged on these topics is to find a movie or podcast that continues the themes of the amendments—showing your kids how other people have thought about these issues in more artistic mediums. Also remember that this is a long game, there is no need to get through everything in one or even 10 sittings! You've got all of childhood to get to these topics.

Unlike the first 10 amendments, many of the additional ones solved one issue rather than creating a set of rights for the people—though some also do that. When describing each amendment, I provide the date of ratification, offer brief remarks on what precipitated the amendment, and, when possible, provide information on more current controversies that might be interesting to discuss with your children.

Eleventh Amendment

The Judicial power of the United States shall not be construed to extend to any suit in law or equity, commenced or prosecuted against one of the United States by Citizens of another State, or by Citizens or Subjects of any Foreign State.

Ratified February 7, 1795 (seven years after the Constitution)

This amendment states that citizens of one state cannot sue the governments of another state and that no citizens or subjects of any foreign state can sue the United States. The greater concept is known as sovereign immunity. When talking to your kids about this one, consider how diplomats enjoy immunity and cannot be prosecuted for most actions while serving abroad. Ask them what they'd do if they could have the same sort of protections if they were representing their country abroad.

The concepts underlying this amendment had been bandied about since the time of ratification, but a series of court cases working through their way through the federal system in the late 1700s made the need for Congressional action clear. The relevance today of this amendment for most children is minor, but it does show how the branches of government interact. When the courts ruled in a way that Congress did not agree with, they were able to use the amendment process to change the rules to work in their favor.

Twelfth Amendment

The Electors shall meet in their respective states and vote by ballot for President and Vice-President, one of whom, at least, shall not be an inhabitant of the same state with themselves; they shall name in their ballots the person voted for as President, and in distinct ballots the person voted for as Vice-President, and they shall make distinct lists of all persons voted for as President, and of all persons voted for as Vice-President, and of the number of votes for each, which lists they shall sign and certify, and transmit sealed to the seat of the government of the United States, directed to the President of the Senate; – The President of the Senate shall, in the presence of the Senate and House of Representatives, open all the certificates and the votes shall then be counted; – The person having the greatest number of votes for President, shall be the President, if such number be a majority of the whole number of Electors appointed; and if no person have such majority, then from the persons having the highest numbers not exceeding three on the list of those voted for as President, the House of Representatives shall choose immediately, by ballot, the President. But in choosing the President, the votes shall be taken by states, the representation from each state having one vote; a quorum for this purpose shall consist of a member or members from two-thirds of the states, and a majority of all the states shall be necessary to a choice. And if the House of Representatives shall not choose a President whenever the right of choice shall devolve upon them, before the fourth day of March next following, then the Vice-President shall act as President, as in case of the death or other constitutional disability of the President. – The person having the greatest number of votes as Vice-President, shall be the Vice-President, if such number be a majority of the whole number of Electors appointed, and if no person have a majority, then from the two highest numbers on the list, the Senate shall choose the Vice-President; a quorum for the purpose shall consist of *two-thirds of the whole number of Senators, and a majority of the whole number shall be necessary to a choice. But no person constitutionally ineligible to the office of President shall be eligible to that of Vice-President of the United States.*

Ratified June 15, 1804 (16 years after the Constitution)

The 1800 presidential election was conducted under different rules than we have today. States chose electors through various methods, including popular vote or legislative appointment. Electors voted for two presidential candidates, with the runner-up becoming vice president. This system led to a tie in 1800 due to multiple candidates running. The candidates you are likely to know were Thomas Jefferson, John Adams, and Aaron Burr.

Jefferson won against Adams with a 73–65 electoral vote. However, due to the same-ticket voting, both Jefferson and his running mate, Aaron Burr, ended up with equal votes. The Constitution mandates that in such a tie, the House of Representatives decides the president, with each state casting one vote. After 36 ballots, Jefferson was chosen as president.

The amendment revised the electoral process to ensure separate votes for president and vice president. This change took effect in 1804. The custom of presidential candidates selecting running mates from the same party began around the Civil War (1861–1865) and became standard practice post-war, with states aligning ballots accordingly.

The amendment provides for a contingency when no presidential candidate secures a majority in the Electoral College. In such cases, the House selects the president from the top three candidates, with each state casting one vote. If they can't decide, the vice president assumes the presidency. Similarly, if no vice presidential candidate wins a majority, the Senate chooses between the top two. Additionally, the amendment clarifies that the vice president must meet all presidential eligibility criteria.

After this amendment, it would be over 60 years before any changes to the Constitution were adopted, with the Thirteenth, Fourteenth, and Fifteenth Amendments all being considered at the conclusion of the American Civil War.

Thirteenth Amendment

Section 1

Neither slavery nor involuntary servitude, except as a punishment for crime whereof the party shall have been duly convicted, shall exist within the United States, or any place subject to their jurisdiction.

Section 2

Congress shall have power to enforce this article by appropriate legislation.

Ratified December 6, 1865 (77 years after the Constitution)

The Thirteenth Amendment, passed after the Civil War, formally abolished slavery and involuntary servitude in the United States, except as punishment for a crime. It also empowered Congress to pass laws to enforce this ban, as legislators anticipated resistance in changing their ways from former slave states. The Thirteenth Amendment's exception for involuntary servitude as punishment for a crime was accepted when enacted by legislators from both the North and the South. However, it became a tool for states to control freed slaves through biased laws known as Black codes and Jim Crow policies, perpetuating racial injustice.

There are a great number of conversations you can have with your children on the topic of slavery. Discussing slavery with children can involve reflecting on your family's past and considering different historical perspectives. Ask where your ancestors were in the 1800s. Were they enslaved, slave owners, neither? Had they established themselves in the United States, or did they immigrate later?

Some parents have expressed hesitancy in talking about these topics because they don't want their children to feel familial shame about something they don't control. But children usually appreciate understanding historical progress and how their ancestors' choices shape society. You can talk about this topic while acknowledging past mistakes and emphasizing that kids today obviously didn't cause those things, but it's important for them to think about them and how decisions from the past influence things today. Kids—especially teens—love feeling like they know better, or that they do things better than their parents and grandparents did.

This conversation is likely not the only one you'll have about race and U.S. politics with your family. Depending on your own situation and history, you'll have a chance to walk through what you think your family got right or wrong, and what sorts of injustices or privileges might have been afforded them based on race and time. The Thirteenth, Fourteenth, and Fifteenth Amendments offer a way to have these discussion in the context of government decision-making rather than through a framework of personal judgment, and that distance may make an otherwise difficult conversation a little bit easier.

Many authors have taken on the issue of equal rights and racism in the United States. For you as adults, if you wish to learn more about the Thirteenth, Fourteenth, and Fifteenth Amendments and how states and the federal government responded in subsequent decades, I recommend *The Color of Law: A Forgotten History of How Our Government Segregated America* by Richard Rothstein and Michelle Alexander's *The New Jim Crow: Mass Incarceration in the Age of Colorblindness*.

There are numerous books and resources to help children understand slavery's impact on the United States. Schools often provide a historical context; your children may already know something about slavery, but some schools are moving away from teaching this subject as a part of history lessons. When going through our central governing documents, however, it's a part that can't be skipped.

These topics can be painful but using age-appropriate books can be a way to make things easier and more approachable for younger kids. For your youngest readers, the illustrated book *Many Thousand Gone* by Virginia Hamilton covers a lot of ground and does so in a straight-talking and engaging way. For 8- to 12-year-olds, *If You Lived When There Was Slavery in America* by Anne Kamma does a good job of describing the realities of life in that time, which can be hard for children of today to grasp. For older teens you may wish to watch rather than read something with them so that you can experience it together and discuss things in real time. The documentary *13th* directed by Ava DuVernay and available on streaming services can be a way to take on some of the harder details of slavery, the Thirteenth Amendment, and current-day challenges together.

Fourteenth Amendment

Section 1

All persons born or naturalized in the United States, and subject to the jurisdiction thereof, are citizens of the United States and of the State wherein they reside. No State shall make or enforce any law which shall abridge the privileges or immunities of citizens of the United States; nor shall any State deprive any person of life, liberty, or property, without due process of law; nor deny to any person within its jurisdiction the equal protection of the laws.

Section 2

Representatives shall be apportioned among the several States according to their respective numbers, counting the whole number of persons in each State, excluding Indians not taxed. But when the right to vote at any election for the choice of electors for President and Vice-President of the United States, Representatives in Congress, the Executive and Judicial officers of a State, or the members of the Legislature thereof, is denied to any of the male inhabitants of such State, being twenty-one years of age, and citizens of the United States, or in any way abridged, except for participation in rebellion, or other crime, the basis of representation therein shall be reduced in the proportion which the number of such male citizens shall bear to the whole number of male citizens twenty-one years of age in such State.

Section 3

No person shall be a Senator or Representative in Congress, or elector of President and Vice-President, or hold any office, civil or military, under the United States, or under any State, who, having previously taken an oath, as a member of Congress, or as an officer of the United States, or as a member of any State legislature, or as an executive or judicial officer of any State, to support the Constitution of the United States, shall have engaged in insurrection or rebellion against the same, or given aid or comfort to the enemies thereof. But Congress may by a vote of two-thirds of each House, remove such disability.

Section 4

The validity of the public debt of the United States, authorized by law, including debts incurred for payment of pensions and bounties for services in suppressing insurrection or rebellion, shall not be questioned. But neither the United States nor any State shall assume or pay any debt or obligation incurred in aid of insurrection or rebellion against the United States, or any claim for the loss or emancipation of any slave; but all such debts, obligations and claims shall be held illegal and void.

Section 5

The Congress shall have the power to enforce, by appropriate legislation, the provisions of this article.

Ratified July 9, 1868 (80 years after the Constitution)

The amendment guarantees citizenship and equal protection under the law to all, specifically addressing the legal status of newly freed Black people and preventing states from enacting laws that would create routes to second-class citizenship. It ensures life, liberty, and property cannot be taken without due process.

Section 1 of this amendment is related to multiple current controversies that may be areas of interest for you or your children. It guarantees birthright citizenship, which was necessary for ensuring that former slaves and their descendants were recognized as citizens. Birthright citizenship today is typically discussed through the lens of babies born within the United States to parents who are not themselves citizens.

The second section of the Fourteenth Amendment revised representation in Congress by counting the full population of each state, "excluding Indians not taxed,"[9] and affirmed the voting rights of all male citizens over 21, except those penalized for rebellion or crimes. It threatened to reduce a state's congressional representation if it unlawfully abridged men's voting rights. Efforts to enforce this via penalizing poll tax states in 1870 were hampered by political disputes over enforcement and criteria for rights infringements.[10] The Fourteenth Amendment marked the first constitutional reference to voter gender, affirming men's right to vote. Discussing this with your family can lead to broader conversations on gender and societal changes in perceptions of rights and equality.

The third section of the Fourteenth Amendment bars individuals who supported insurrection or rebellion against the United States from holding public office unless two-thirds of Congress votes to lift the ban individually. A broad amnesty was extended in 1872, except for key Confederate figures like Jefferson Davis and Robert E. Lee.[11] This clause recently had a moment in U.S. politics as different states have cited it when determining whether or not to allow former President Donald Trump—who stands accused of inciting different forms of antigovernment uprisings on January 6, 2021—on the ballot for president. Knowing that states retain the right to administer elections, our state and federal courts had to wrestle with some very complicated parts of constitutional law.

The fourth section deals with how debts incurred during the Civil War and subsequent claims are to be handled at the federal level.

Finally, section five gives Congress the ability to enforce any of the above through legislation.

Fifteenth Amendment

Section 1

The right of citizens of the United States to vote shall not be denied or abridged by the United States or by any State on account of race, color, or previous condition of servitude.

Section 2

The Congress shall have the power to enforce this article by appropriate legislation.

Ratified February 3, 1870 (82 years after the Constitution)

The final post–Civil War amendment directly addresses voting rights. The Fourteenth Amendment implies that all men over 21 are entitled to vote, and the Fifteenth Amendment makes it so.

The amendment stipulates that voting rights cannot be limited based on race, color, or past servitude, using "citizen" rather than "man," but the interpretation was that this phrasing meant men only. Recall everyone voting and serving in the federal government and nearly everyone serving and voting in state and local positions were men at this time.

When teaching children about voting rights, explain how the Fifteenth, Nineteenth, Twenty-third, and Twenty-sixth

Amendments widened voting access. Discuss historical and current voting exclusions, like noncitizens or felons. Debate the criteria for voting eligibility and the implications of different laws. Engage older teens by questioning the voting age versus driving age, turning the conversation to the judgment placed on different age-related responsibilities.

Sixteenth Amendment

The Congress shall have power to lay and collect taxes on incomes, from whatever source derived, without apportionment among the several States, and without regard to any census or enumeration.

Ratified February 3, 1913 (125 years after the Constitution)

The Sixteenth Amendment authorizes the federal government to collect income taxes. Taxes are an interesting starting point for discussion, because though not everyone has to vote or even register to vote, everyone in the United States is subject to paying taxes.

Use the "dessert tax" analogy to teach kids about taxes. If you buy them an ice cream sundae, taking a bite as "tax" shows that while they enjoy the treat, part of it supports the provider—the parent—much like taxes fund communal services. This is obviously not how taxes work, but it can start a larger conversation. I described taxes to my daughter in the following way. I earn income as a professor, and I pay the government taxes on the income. I busted out 100 pennies to show the percentage that I take home versus what I send to the government in taxes. At this point in the exercise, it still seemed unfair to her.

Then I told her that everyone who works a job must do the same thing, so in the end the government has a good deal of collective money it pooled from each of us. And at this point, she asked, "Why? Why do they get to do that?" And then I walked through all the collective things I needed in order to work at this job in the first place.

For me to be working in this job, I had to do a lot of hard things on my own, but I also benefited from many things that were the result of efforts that were coordinated and sometimes carried out by the government. I explained the benefits I received: public education, clean water, safe food, roads, medicine safety, and environmental protection. These collective goods, funded by taxes, enhance our community and country, and my life allowing me to be where I am today. I also pointed out that she too benefits from them.

You can create your own list of public services that benefit you, just as you might identify government spending based on tax revenues you disagree with or consider wasteful. It's good to discuss both the positive and negative aspects of government with your children, remaining factual and calm, and to appreciate the complexity of governance and the importance of electing competent officials to manage our tax dollars.

Seventeenth Amendment

The Senate of the United States shall be composed of two Senators from each State, elected by the people thereof, for six years; and each Senator shall have one vote. The electors in each State shall have the qualifications requisite for electors of the most numerous branch of the State legislatures.

> *When vacancies happen in the representation of any State in the Senate, the executive authority of such State shall issue writs of election to fill such vacancies: Provided, That the legislature of any State may empower the executive thereof to make temporary appointments until the people fill the vacancies by election as the legislature may direct.*
>
> *This amendment shall not be so construed as to affect the election or term of any Senator chosen before it becomes valid as part of the Constitution.*
>
> Ratified April 8, 1913 (125 years after the Constitution)

The Seventeenth Amendment, effective after 1913, allowed citizens to directly vote for their federal senators. Spurred by calls for more transparent government, this amendment shifted the election of senators from state legislatures to a direct vote by the people, just like how representatives are elected. The amendment also allowed governors to call an election or appoint a temporary replacement for a vacant Senate seat until the next regularly scheduled election.

Discuss with older children how the Seventeenth Amendment influences party politics and senatorial appointments by presidents. Presidents prefer appointing senators from their own party, who are likely to be replaced by similarly aligned individuals by governors of the same party. This allows for political alignment but can have unpredictable longer-term effects on party control. For example, when Joe Biden chose Kamala Harris as his vice presidential candidate, he anticipated that California's Democratic governor would appoint a Democrat to her Senate seat, which is exactly what happened. Conversely, Donald Trump's appointment of Jeff Sessions as Attorney General led to a temporary Republican replacement, but in the subsequent election a Democrat won the seat, illustrating the uncertain nature of such a strategy and the fluidity of politics.

Eighteenth Amendment

Section 1

After one year from the ratification of this article the manufacture, sale, or transportation of intoxicating liquors within, the importation thereof into, or the exportation thereof from the United States and all territory subject to the jurisdiction thereof for beverage purposes is hereby prohibited.

Section 2

The Congress and the several States shall have concurrent power to enforce this article by appropriate legislation.

Section 3

This article shall be inoperative unless it shall have been ratified as an amendment to the Constitution by the legislatures of the several States, as provided in the Constitution, within seven years from the date of the submission hereof to the States by the Congress.

Ratified January 16, 1919 (131 years after the Constitution)

The Eighteenth Amendment, known as Prohibition, banned the production, sale, and transport of alcoholic beverages in the United States. It's the first amendment that had a ratification time limit and it also gave states the power to enact their own enforcement laws.

When it comes to discussing the Prohibition era with your older children, it can open a dialogue about government and other complex topics like drugs and alcohol. You can ask your kids what factors a government should consider in order to completely prohibit a substance. Are there any substances today that a government might be justified in banning? The Prohibition era has inspired many creative works, so if your family enjoys bonding over movies, you could explore films related to that period. However, keep in mind that these themes are often more adult-oriented, often involving organized crime violence. Therefore, it's advisable to preview them before watching as a family.

Nineteenth Amendment

The right of citizens of the United States to vote shall not be denied or abridged by the United States or by any State on account of sex.

Congress shall have power to enforce this article by appropriate legislation.

Ratified August 18, 1920 (132 years after the Constitution)

Shortly after Prohibition was enacted, women throughout the United States gained the right to vote. Women in certain states already had voting rights before the amendment. Wyoming led the way in 1869 by granting women the right to vote, followed by Colorado, Utah, and Idaho in 1909.[12] Women in newly settled frontier states achieved voting rights earlier due to the unique demands and circumstances of their lives. Unlike women in the earliest settled colonies, they enjoyed more parity with men since the challenges of traveling and settling in new territories didn't align with traditional gender roles.

Women's right to vote was a significant step, yet full citizenship rights lagged. Even after 1920—and in some ways until very recently—women faced hurdles in being allowed to serve on juries and in the military. In 1961, the Supreme Court in *Hoyt v. Florida* upheld women's exclusion from jury duty, citing domestic roles as justification. Only in 1975, with *Taylor v. Louisiana*, did women gain full jury duty inclusion. The 1948 Armed Services Integration Act allowed women into the military, but it wasn't until 1975 that all military academies admitted women, and wasn't until 2013 that women were permitted to serve in combat roles.

These historical milestones provide a valuable context for discussing the Nineteenth Amendment and women's rights with your children. Additionally, they help us understand how societal views have changed about what it means to be a citizen.

Twentieth Amendment

Section 1

The terms of the President and the Vice President shall end at noon on the 20th day of January, and the terms of Senators and Representatives at noon on the 3d day of January, of the years in which such terms would have ended if this article had not been ratified; and the terms of their successors shall then begin.

Section 2

The Congress shall assemble at least once in every year, and such meeting shall begin at noon on the 3d day of January, unless they shall by law appoint a different day.

Section 3

If, at the time fixed for the beginning of the term of the President, the President elect shall have died, the Vice President elect shall become President. If a President shall not have been chosen before the time fixed for the beginning of his term, or if the President elect shall have failed to qualify, then the Vice President elect shall act as President until a President shall have qualified; and the Congress may by law provide for the case wherein neither a President elect nor a Vice President shall have qualified, declaring who shall then act as President, or the manner in which one who is to act shall be selected, and such person shall act accordingly until a President or Vice President shall have qualified.

Section 4

The Congress may by law provide for the case of the death of any of the persons from whom the House of Representatives may choose a President whenever the right of choice shall have devolved upon them, and for the case of the death of any of the persons from whom the Senate may choose a Vice President whenever the right of choice shall have devolved upon them.

Section 5

Sections 1 and 2 shall take effect on the 15th day of October following the ratification of this article.

Section 6

This article shall be inoperative unless it shall have been ratified as an amendment to the Constitution by the legislatures of three-fourths of the several States within seven years from the date of its submission.

Ratified January 23, 1933 (145 years after the Constitution)

The Twentieth Amendment streamlines the transition of power, sets specific dates for the start of new terms, and guarantees that Congress convenes at least once a year. It also provides contingency plans in case of election complications.

The amendment fine-tunes the federal government's schedule, setting new terms to start on January 20 for the president and January 3 for Congress, ensuring a shorter lapse between Election Day and the commencement of official duties. If these dates fall on weekends, the swearing in is moved to the next weekday. Prior to this, people were elected in November but didn't take office until March. That made sense when travel took much longer as it had to happen via horse and would be most difficult during the winter months. By 1933, we had many more transportation options available to newly elected members, and the hassle of traveling in the winter was far less than it was in the 1700 and 1800s.

This amendment outlines procedures for unforeseen events such as the death of an elected candidate between Election Day and Inauguration Day. If a president-elect dies, the vice president-elect becomes president. If no president or vice president is chosen, for instance, due to an Electoral College deadlock, Congress is empowered to appoint an acting president until the impasse is resolved—the House selecting the president and the Senate the vice president. This amendment also had a seven-year ratification limit like the Eighteenth Amendment.

Twenty-first Amendment

Section 1

The eighteenth article of amendment to the Constitution of the United States is hereby repealed.

Section 2

The transportation or importation into any State, Territory, or Possession of the United States for delivery or use therein of intoxicating liquors, in violation of the laws thereof, is hereby prohibited.

Section 3

This article shall be inoperative unless it shall have been ratified as an amendment to the Constitution by conventions in the several States, as provided in the Constitution, within seven years from the date of the submission hereof to the States by the Congress.

Ratified December 5, 1933 (145 years after the Constitution)

The Twenty-first Amendment is very simple: it repealed the Eighteenth Amendment that prohibited the manufacturing, sale, transport, export, and import of alcohol intended for drinking purposes. As in the Eighteenth and Twentieth Amendments, this too had the seven-year ratification time limit.

Twenty-second Amendment

Section 1

No person shall be elected to the office of the President more than twice, and no person who has held the office of President, or acted as President, for more than two years of a term to which some other person was elected President shall be elected to the office of President more than once. But this Article shall not apply to any person holding the office of President when this Article was proposed by Congress, and shall not prevent any person who may be holding the office of President, or acting as President, during the term within which this Article becomes operative from holding the office of President or acting as President during the remainder of such term.

Section 2

This article shall be inoperative unless it shall have been ratified as an amendment to the Constitution by the legislatures of three-fourths of the several States within seven years from the date of its submission to the States by the Congress.

Ratified February 27, 1951 (163 years after the Constitution)

Originally, presidents customarily served only two terms. However, the Constitution did not set term limits for the presidency until after Franklin D. Roosevelt was elected for a third and fourth term. His unprecedented four terms led to the Twenty-second Amendment, which limits a president to two elected terms and a maximum of 10 years in office, accounting for a possibility that a vice president takes over the presidency with two or fewer years left on a term and then wishes to run for two full terms.

This amendment is the only federal term limit. Congress members do not have such restrictions. State and local governments vary; some have term limits to encourage new perspectives, while others do not, citing the benefits of experienced leadership. Something I've learned is that in a classroom just mentioning the phrase "term limits" can spark debates. This sort of topic is ideal for involving older children, especially because they tend to hold views that everyone in politics is too old, and it would be a better place if younger people had more influence. As a family, consider compiling a list of advantages and disadvantages to understand different viewpoints for and against term limits. Like many aspects of politics and government, there is no definitive "right" answer.

Twenty-third Amendment

Section 1

The District constituting the seat of Government of the United States shall appoint in such manner as Congress may direct:

A number of electors of President and Vice President equal to the whole number of Senators and Representatives in Congress to which the District would be entitled if it were a State, but in no event more than the least populous State; they shall be in addition to those appointed by the States, but they shall be considered, for the purposes of the election of President and Vice President, to be electors appointed by a State; and they shall meet in the District and perform such duties as provided by the twelfth article of amendment.

Section 2

The Congress shall have power to enforce this article by appropriate legislation.

Ratified March 29, 1961 (173 years after the Constitution)

The Twenty-third Amendment granted Washington DC residents the right to vote in presidential elections, awarding them three electors in the Electoral College, equal to the least populous state, despite having no voting representatives in Congress. This meant that until 1961, residents of DC had no way to vote in presidential elections. Today, there are nearly 700,000 people living in Washington DC, which is more than the number of people who currently live in Wyoming and Vermont individually.

Though a win for the residents of DC, 3.7 million U.S. territory residents remain unable to vote for president. Congress's nonvoting delegates from Puerto Rico (population 3,285,874), Guam (population 168,485), the U.S. Virgin Islands (population 106,325), the Northern Mariana Islands (population 51,433), and American Samoa (population 49,437) can introduce legislation but not vote on it, nor do these territories participate in the Electoral College. These circumstances offer a way into family discussions on political equity and citizenship.

Twenty-fourth Amendment

Section 1

The right of citizens of the United States to vote in any primary or other election for President or Vice President, for electors for President or Vice President, or for Senator or Representative in Congress, shall not be denied or abridged by the United States or any State by reason of failure to pay poll tax or other tax.

Section 2

The Congress shall have power to enforce this article by appropriate legislation.

Ratified January 23, 1964 (176 years after the Constitution)

The Twenty-fourth Amendment abolished poll taxes in federal elections, removing a barrier that many states used to discriminate against certain voters based on class, race, and gender.

In the post–Civil War South, all states of the former Confederacy implemented some form of a "Poll Tax" or fee-to-vote system. Poll Taxes were instituted in a seemingly neutral manner but effectively disenfranchised poorer voters, especially those affected by slavery's economic legacy. This practice also targeted women, reflecting their exclusion from economic opportunities. These poll taxes were fixed amounts, which meant that their relative value varied depending on someone's income. For instance, a $1 voting fee had a vastly different impact on someone earning $6,300 per year (the average income of white males in the 1960s) compared to someone earning $3,700 (the average income of Black males in the 1960s), $2,500 (the average income of white females in the 1960s), or $2,000 (the average income of Black females in the 1960s).[13]

It's worth noting that the Twenty-fourth Amendment was ratified nearly a century after the Fifteenth Amendment guaranteed Black men the right to vote. When discussing voting equality, consider checking out books and historical narratives that reveal the struggles for suffrage throughout U.S. history. Here are a few that you or your children might enjoy:

- *Bending Toward Justice: The Voting Rights Act and the Transformation of American Democracy* (2013) by Gary May.
- *Give Us the Ballot: The Modern Struggle for Voting Rights in America* (2015) by Ari Berman.
- *The Fight to Vote* (2016) by Michael Waldman.
- *One Person, No Vote: How Voter Suppression Is Destroying Our Democracy* (2018) by Carol Anderson.

Twenty-fifth Amendment

Section 1

In case of the removal of the President from office or of his death or resignation, the Vice President shall become President.

Section 2

Whenever there is a vacancy in the office of the Vice President, the President shall nominate a Vice President who shall take office upon confirmation by a majority vote of both Houses of Congress.

Section 3

Whenever the President transmits to the President pro tempore of the Senate and the Speaker of the House of Representatives his written declaration that he is unable to discharge the powers and duties of his office, and until he transmits to them a written declaration to the contrary, such powers and duties shall be discharged by the Vice President as Acting President.

Section 4

Whenever the Vice President and a majority of either the principal officers of the executive departments or of such other body as Congress may by law provide, transmit to the President pro tempore of the Senate and the Speaker of the House of Representatives their written declaration that the President is unable to discharge the powers and duties of his office, the Vice President shall immediately assume the powers and duties of the office as Acting President.

Thereafter, when the President transmits to the President pro tempore of the Senate and the Speaker of the House of Representatives his written declaration that no inability exists, he shall resume the powers and duties of his office unless the Vice President and a majority of either the principal officers of the executive department or of such other body as Congress may by law provide, transmit within four days to the President pro tempore of the Senate and the Speaker of the House of Representatives their written declaration that the President is unable to discharge the powers and duties of his office. Thereupon Congress shall decide the issue, assembling within forty-eight hours for that purpose if not in session. If the Congress, within twenty-one days after receipt of the latter written declaration, or, if Congress is not in session, within twenty-one days after Congress is required to assemble, determines by two-thirds vote of both Houses that the President is unable to discharge the powers and duties of his office, the Vice President shall continue to discharge the same as Acting President; otherwise, the President shall resume the powers and duties of his office.

Ratified February 10, 1967 (179 years after the Constitution)

The Twenty-fifth Amendment, ratified in 1967, clarified presidential succession and disability procedures, following a history of presidential assassinations, assassination attempts, and incapacitations. It established that the vice president becomes president if the presidency is vacated and allows the president to nominate a new vice president, subject to Congressional approval, if that office becomes empty because a vice president dies or steps down. The third section allows a president to transfer duties to the vice president temporarily, for situations like surgery. In that sort of scenario, the vice president serves as acting president until the president is ready to resume authority—after the anesthesia has worn off and they are sufficiently recovered and capable of resuming the job.

The fourth section describes a process for the removal of a president deemed unfit for office due to incapacitation. This includes a method for the president to fight such a determination—meaning that there could be a disagreement between the president and the vice president and others close to him about his ability to hold the office. If the vice president and a majority of the cabinet—or another body appointed by Congress—judge the president incapable of serving, the vice president steps in as acting president. The president can contest this by declaring that he is capable to the Senate president pro tempore and the House Speaker. If the vice president and the cabinet persist, Congress decides the issue. A two-thirds vote in both houses is needed to keep the vice president in charge; otherwise, the president resumes their duties.

The Twenty-fifth Amendment's final sections haven't been fully used but were a topic of punditry toward the end of the Trump administration. Temporary power transfers *have* occurred during presidents' medical procedures both presidents George W. Bush and Joe Biden temporarily permitted their vice presidents to ascend to the presidency while they underwent colonoscopies.

Discussing this amendment with kids offers historical context into U.S. governance during periods of political uncertainty. It helps children understand the importance of a planned line of succession and the vice president's role. It also opens conversations about presidential fitness and the delicate balance between a leader's health and their duties—something that continues to be a pressing consideration as we continue to elect leaders who are in their 70s and older.

Twenty-sixth Amendment

Section 1

The right of citizens of the United States, who are eighteen years of age or older, to vote shall not be denied or abridged by the United States or by any State on account of age.

Section 2

The Congress shall have power to enforce this article by appropriate legislation.

Ratified July 1, 1971 (183 years after the Constitution)

The Twenty-sixth Amendment is significant for those nearing 18, as it lowered the voting age from 21 to 18 nationwide. Enacted during the Vietnam War era, it addressed the argument that if 18-year-olds could serve in the military, they should also be able to vote. This reasoning, dating back to World War II, eventually garnered enough support to change the law.

Today, the 18- to 24-year-old demographic is the least likely to vote. Young people's perspectives are often underrepresented in politics, and their mobile lifestyles, such as attending college or relocating, can hinder their voter registration. Encourage your child to prioritize voter registration with each move, alongside other essentials like utilities and internet setup.

Twenty-seventh Amendment

No law, varying the compensation for the services of the Senators and Representatives, shall take effect, until an election of representatives shall have intervened.

Ratified May 7, 1992 (204 years after the Constitution)

The last amendment to our Constitution, which came into force in 1992, tells an interesting story of persistence and offers a lesson that is consistent with the theme of this book. It addresses congressional pay, stipulating that any salary changes voted by Congress can only take effect after the next election, ensuring lawmakers cannot immediately benefit from their own legislation regarding pay increases.

Proposed with the original Bill of Rights, it lingered unratified for over two centuries. Rediscovered by student Gregory Watson in 1982, he realized its ratification was still possible and began a campaign for its adoption. By 1992, the required number of states had ratified it, illustrating the impact one person's resolve can have on the nation's laws. This story highlights the influence individuals, including the youth, can wield in our democracy.

Conclusion

This chapter was long, but I know that if you've made it through, you now know so much more about our government than most adults. Having fluency with the Constitution should be a minimum of our educational system, but we know that it's not. By taking it upon yourself to learn more and by pledging to talk about these things with your kids, you're giving them a leg up on life. They will be less likely to fall prey to outrageous headlines, more able to discern why things happen in the way they do, and more capable themselves to entering a system with the hopes of changing things.

The Constitution spells out the federal government structure. Each state has a constitution of their own, oftentimes longer than this one and more detailed. Though useful to know and read through once, something that can be easier to keep in mind is which level of government is responsible for what. That's the focus of the next chapter.

Notes

1. See National Archives. (n.d.). The Constitution of the United States. https://www.archives.gov/founding-docs/constitution-transcript.

2. Library of Congress. (n.d.). Digital collections. https://www.loc.gov/collections/.

3. The non-voting delegates come from Washington DC, Puerto Rico, Guam, the Northern Mariana Islands, the U.S. Virgin Islands, American Samoa. Interestingly, the 4,347,736 people of DC, Puerto Rico, Guam, the Northern Mariana Islands, U.S. Virgin Islands, and American Samoa have no voting representation in Congress, but the 4,609,028 people of Wyoming, Vermont, Alaska, North Dakota, South Dakota, Delaware have 18 members of Congress.

4. *Clinton v. City of New York*, 524 U.S. 417 (1998).

5. There is also a recognition that some vacancies may need appointments in a faster timeline than when the Senate may be able to consider a nominee. In those rare instances the president has the ability to make what is known as a "recess appointment" by appointing a person for a time until the Senate returns from a period of adjournment, also known as recess, to consider the nominee fully.

6. Konig, D.T. (2008). Why the Second Amendment has a preamble: Original public meaning and the political culture of written Constitutions in Revolutionary American. *UCLA Law Review* 56: 1295.

7. Shusterman, N. (2020). *Armed Citizens: The Road from Ancient Rome to the Second Amendment*. Charlottesville, VA: University of Virginia Press.

8. It's important to note that this right does not extend to individuals serving in the armed forces.

9. The status and treatment of Native Americans in the United States is often unclear and inconsistently handled over time. For a deeper look at this subject contextual to the time of the Fourteenth Amendment see Tennant, B. (2011). "Excluding Indians not taxed": "Dred Scott, Standing Bear, Elk" and the legal status of Native Americans in the latter half of the nineteenth century. *International Social Science Review* 86(1/2): 24–43.

10. For a thorough look at the Fourteenth Amendment and some of its shortcomings see Curtis, M.K. (2007). The Fourteenth Amendment: Recalling what the court forgot. *Drake Law Review* 56: 911.

11. For more on amnesty granting using the Fourteenth Amendment see Magliocca, G.N. (2021). Amnesty and section three of the Fourteenth Amendment. *36 Constitutional Commentary 87*.

12. And there are a few earlier examples of states that permitted women to vote, like in New Jersey where propertied, unmarried, or widowed women could vote as early as 1776 before the right was taken away in 1807.

13. U.S. Census Bureau. (2021). Current population survey, 1968 to 2021, Annual social and economic supplements (CPS ASEC).

8

Federalism and Who Is Responsible for What

During the process of writing this book, I spoke with numerous educators who highlighted *federalism* as one of the most misunderstood aspects of the U.S. government. Federalism is straightforward but requires understanding the different roles at each government level. Teaching kids about federalism early demystifies how government works, and like any complicated topic, it's easier if you get started early.

Federalism is a foundational concept of U.S. governance where power is shared between the federal government and the states and local governments. The idea of split and shared governance across different levels was front and center during the formation of the Constitution. The system was designed to balance a strong federal presence with state sovereignty—which were two of the things wanted by different sets of founders. This balance allows for a distribution of responsibilities—big-picture issues like national defense fall under federal jurisdiction, while states and local governments address community-specific needs like education and public services.

This layered approach is meant to allow for a more functional government because decisions can be made at an appropriate level, depending on the scale of the issue. For example, during the COVID-19 pandemic, the federal government handled national strategies such as policies on vaccine development and processing travelers and immigrants; states managed vaccine distribution and came up with systems for securing the rights of people and businesses amid an unfolding health crisis; and local entities decided on school policies and how to deploy first responders. Though one might quibble with a choice made at a specific level, it is a strength of our system to have adaptable forms of government that can make policy choices based on the specific needs of the people of a state or locality.

Appreciating who does what in government helps us make sense of politics. It's illuminating for your kids to learn that even the most powerful person in the country, the president, does not have the authority to address certain issues, like the start time of their school. Understanding federalism clarifies governmental roles, which is important because our national media would have many people believe that "politics" is just about national headlines. It's not. State and local politics, where much of the impactful decision-making happens, often operates more collaboratively and with direct community involvement. By knowing the differences across levels, you and children should have a way to think of political participation and the potential for change as something that is more tangible and less intimidating or overwhelming.

By exploring federalism with your family, you can better navigate the policy issues and political landscape that matter most to you. By reviewing the roles of government at all levels, I hope you and your family can better see through the national political drama and instead be encouraged to take greater note of your state and local politics.

Divisions of Government Powers

The Tenth Amendment clarifies that powers not given to the federal government belong to the states or the people. State legislatures, working with governors, address a range of topics such as transportation, funding for state departments and programs, licensing and permitting laws, criminal statutes, family matters, business contracts, workers' compensation, real estate, agriculture, and education guidelines specific to their respective states. Many aspects of our lives are shaped by state-level legislators and executives rather than federal lawmakers. Local governments handle immediate community needs, such as public services, zoning, and local ordinances, shaping our daily environment and quality of life.

Federal System

The U.S. federal government is the top level of government with one central administration headed by the president, with appointed members leading the other parts of the executive branch. Congress, our national legislature, is split into the House and Senate and made up of elected representatives and senators from every state in the nation. The federal judiciary has three levels: district courts for trials, appellate courts for appeals after trials, and the Supreme Court at the top to consider a few cases in which they have original jurisdiction and many more cases on appeal.

This highest level of government manages issues spanning the entire nation, like foreign policy. Federal laws affect all states, unlike state or local laws, which are jurisdiction specific, meaning that they only apply within the geography of their own governments. A helpful discussion with your kids could be about the reach of federal responsibilities. Big, nationwide concerns? That's federal. More localized matters? Look to state or local governments. You can ask them what areas of society they wish would be different and then think about who is responsible for laws at that level on that subject.

While the president, Congress, and Supreme Court often get the spotlight, a good deal of federal operations happen within executive agencies. These agencies are staffed by nonelected officials who serve as expert bureaucrats in charge of specific policy areas. Overall, the federal government employs over two million people, with the Department of Defense having the largest share of federal workers. As of 2024, there are over 400 federal entities within the executive branch. Among these, there are 15 main executive departments, each headed by presidential appointees confirmed by the Senate:

- Agriculture
- Commerce
- Defense
- Education
- Energy
- Health and Human Services
- Homeland Security
- Housing and Urban Development
- Interior
- Justice
- Labor
- State
- Transportation
- Treasury
- Veterans Affairs

State Systems

Each of the 50 states and territories in the United States operates its own government, mirroring the federal structure but
with unique traits. Governors head the executive branches, and
most states have bicameral legislatures, except for Nebraska's
single-chamber system. Legislative chambers vary in size, from
Alaska's 40-member House to New Hampshire's 400-member
House, and from Alaska's 20-member Senate to Minnesota's
67 members.

The professionalization of state legislators differs widely.
Being a state legislator in some states is a full-time job with a
salary similar to working in the private sector; in other states,
being a legislator is a part-time position, with lawmakers jug-
gling their legislative duties with regular jobs. Salaries for state
legislators also vary. For instance, New York's state legislators
earn $142,000 annually, whereas New Hampshire's receive just
$100. It can be enlightening to compare the pay and roles of state
legislators across the country with those in your own state—and
when you get upset about something that happens in your state,
think about what the job and pay of a legislator look like—it's
not easy. State legislatures are distinct from the federal Congress,
and though some state legislators will run for federal office, the
actions within state legislature do not really influence what happens at the federal level.

Governors are responsible for implementing and enforcing laws in conjunction with other executive officers at the state
level. Governors serve mostly four-year terms with the exception
of those in New Hampshire and Vermont, both of which have
two-year terms. Term limits vary across the states. The longest-
serving governor was Terry Branstad of Iowa, who was elected
to six nonconsecutive four-year terms starting in 1983—totaling

22 years in office—before resigning in 2017 to become the U.S. ambassador to China. The most stringent term limit is in Virginia, where governors are prohibited from serving consecutive terms and instead must wait until the next governor has served to start a run for another term.

Like the president, governors generally have veto powers over legislation passed by state legislatures, but specific time limits and types of legislation that are eligible to be vetoed vary by state. Governors also enjoy executive order privileges to decree and implement some policies within a limited set of areas. There are different approaches to budgeting across the U.S. states, but in many ways, governors have more budgeting power than the president. Governors' offices can draft state budgets and send them for legislative approval. Some governors enjoy line-item veto privileges on budgets, meaning they can strike specific spending or budgeting provisions that they disagree with. Governors command their state's National Guard for emergencies. They can mobilize the Guard for disaster response, civil unrest, election security. During the COVID-19 pandemic, some governors used the National Guard for testing, delivering personal protective equipment, and vaccine administration.

State executive agencies sometimes collaborate with their federal counterparts. For instance, state law enforcement may work with the Federal Bureau of Investigations (FBI). However, roles are distinct at different levels. This collaborative difference is on display when both federal and state governments want to find tax cheats, but the Internal Revenue Service (IRS) handles federal taxes while state departments of revenue manage state taxes.

Each state has a unique judicial system, with some having specialized courts for family, juvenile, or drug cases. This adaptability is a hallmark of U.S. federalism. Unlike the uniform federal courts, state courts can be quite different, leading to distinct bar exams for each state, although some allow reciprocity for lawyers who pass the test in one state to practice in another.

State–federal cooperation is clear in programs like food assistance, where federal and state agencies partner to ensure services, with the federal government playing a greater role in oversight and during emergencies such as natural disasters, with the state being responsible for more of the day-to-day implementation of such programs.

When discussing policy areas of interest with your children, many of the things they care about are likely regulated at the state or local level. Most school regulations, for example, are determined by state and local governments. Understanding who is responsible for implementing and enforcing these policies is a good starting point for conversations. A quick visit to the National Conference of State Legislatures website can give you a snapshot of how state governments vary. It's a handy tool for staying informed and thinking about the specifics of your own state.

Local Systems

Local governments are different all over the nation, with their structures ranging from state-like systems in large cities to very simple setups in smaller areas. Big cities typically have mayors and elected city councils handling local matters, while smaller towns might use town managers, ombudsmen, or volunteer-based town councils, other unincorporated areas may lack anything that looks like a local government and may instead have to turn to state officials for dealing with their issues.

At the executive level, local positions like agency commissioners in big cities can earn nearly $200,000 annually, and roles like city managers or treasurers often exceed $100,000. Yet, much local government work, including on city or town councils, is volunteer-based. These volunteers, not professionals, manage responsibilities such as overseeing liquor licenses and zoning in community boards or town meetings. Much of this work is done by committee or task force, which require sets of people to meet up regularly outside of normal working hours to hear complaints from their communities and get to work on remedying them.

Local governments run on modest budgets from federal/state funds and local taxes. They handle community matters through committees on the environment, senior services, housing, businesses, and the like. They oversee zoning, building permits, and cultural landmarks. Local arenas like schools and parks are also under their purview. Local officials are often accessible and willing to engage with children, whether by visiting classrooms or hosting them in their offices, though many local officials may not have their own official offices, so you might meet them at public parks or other public spaces.

It's important to recognize the distinction between the various levels of politics. Unlike the national scene, local politics is less partisan and more about practical solutions for a geographically close community. Those serving locally are typically driven by a desire to enhance their immediate surroundings rather than national political agendas.

Specific Issue Areas

Our political system is a partnership between local, state, and federal governments, each with unique duties. Here, I'll outline major issues and their management across these levels. The organization is such that topics primarily dealt with at the federal level are discussed at the beginning of the list, while those closer to the local level are toward the end. However, many issues fall somewhere in between and serve as examples of cooperative or multilayer federalism.

The list is not exhaustive, but it covers the areas that Americans often consider important based on national surveys. I'll give a broad view of these policies, but the specifics for your state or city are yours to discover. This should help you understand and discuss what's important with your children. If you're already familiar with certain topics, feel free to skip ahead; or read through for a full picture to be prepared to answer a wide range of questions from your kids.

National Security and Foreign Policy

Federal Level

The federal government has primary authority over national security and foreign policy, with exclusive powers to negotiate treaties and trade deals globally. Multiple federal agencies aim to safeguard U.S. interests and uphold its values abroad, relying on specialized professionals with deep expertise in both policy areas and specific regions of the world. Many federal departments, including State, Defense, Homeland Security, and more, collaborate in these domains.

These areas involve both home front and global matters, with a good deal of annual federal funding allocated to bolster our security through diplomacy actions and military readiness. National security also extends to immigration and trade. The upkeep of military infrastructure, a federal responsibility, is necessary for these efforts and both parties generally support spending in this area.

Foreign policy is how the United States interacts with the world, from ally collaboration to managing adversaries. Sometimes, it involves engaging with non-ally nations for strategic gains. For example, our relationship with China includes elements of both friendship, particularly in trade, and adversarial dynamics in areas like space, cyber warfare, and human rights.

Both peacetime efforts and conflict decisions require global intelligence gathering. In the legislative branch of government, the House and Senate foreign affairs committees review and influence policy, while the secretary of state leads diplomatic efforts, with the Department of Defense and many smaller entities within both contributing to our efforts.

If your child is interested in foreign policy or national security, encourage them to study the federal agencies and actors responsible for those areas of interest. Knowing more about what different parts of our apparatus are responsible for is a way to make a focused path of understanding for these otherwise complex subjects.

State Level

Article I, Section 10 of the U.S. Constitution limits states' involvement in international affairs, reserving most powers for the federal government. Nevertheless, states can still engage globally, with some having offices for trade or diplomatic missions to promote cultural and technological exchanges with other countries. Border states like those next to Mexico often have unique approaches on border policies due to their location. While immigration policy is set at the federal level, and while our border patrol members are federal workers, they come from state and local communities who experience immigration policy impacts in ways that are different to people who don't live in border states and towns.

Federal, state, and local governments collaborate on national security. The Department of Homeland Security, for example, partners with state and local entities to share intelligence and resources. This is important because local agencies are closer to community-specific issues. Additionally, joint training programs enhance state agencies' capabilities to work with the federal government on security matters.

Local Level

Local governments, while not directly involved in foreign policy, play a key role in national security, particularly through partnerships with federal agencies. A significant concern for local entities is the protection of their information systems, which tend to lack the robust defenses of higher government levels and are therefore vulnerable to cyber threats from international actors. While the local level may not be the main stage for foreign policy and national security, it is still a front for safeguarding against online tech attacks for data loss.

Immigration

Federal Level

Immigration policy is mainly a federal matter, handled by the Department of Homeland Security and the Department of State, which oversee entry laws, visas, and undocumented individuals' cases. Despite this, states have become more active, leading to debates between state and federal authorities, and among political parties.

The U.S. Citizenship and Immigration Services manages the immigration system, a significant task given that immigrants comprise between 10% and 14% of our total population.[1] As a past example of federal action in a federalism context on immigration, President Donald Trump signed an executive order that sought to deny federal funding to sanctuary cities,[2] which are jurisdictions that choose not to cooperate with federal efforts to deport undocumented immigrants. However, this order raised constitutional concerns as it potentially violated federalism principles and could have undermined the separation of powers. By bypassing Congress, such orders could have a dangerous precedent by granting presidents the ability to enforce policies without congressional authorization. In response, the city of San Francisco sued, and eventually U.S. Federal District Judge William H. Orrick issued an injunction to permanently block the order.[3]

The federal government can grant Temporary Protected Status (TPS) to immigrants from troubled countries, allowing them temporary safety without being considered illegal immigrants. An example of this power being used was when President Biden committed to welcome up to 100,000 Ukrainians fleeing Russia's invasion in 2022.[4] This is a power entirely reserved to the federal government, so though people will live in states and towns, the legality of being in the United States is determined at the federal level.

State Level

While the federal government sets immigration policies, states have considerable flexibility in how they comply with and interpret these policies. Some states offer state-level benefits like healthcare to undocumented immigrants, while others may not support asylum seekers, sometimes even transporting them to other states. Between 2022–2023, Texas sent over 42,000 recently arrived immigrants to other states without first coordinating with the destination states. Debate continues over how strictly state and local officials should follow federal immigration laws. Approaches vary; states such as California and Massachusetts grant immigrants certain privileges like driver's licenses and in-state tuition, whereas states like Texas require local law enforcement to collaborate with federal immigration authorities.

And still yet other states restrict police from inquiring about immigration status during stops.

Though policy is set at the federal level, related immigration policies differ significantly across the United States, reflecting each state's values and priorities. For those curious about local immigration laws, resources like the Immigrant Legal Resource Center provide detailed information online.[5]

Local Level

Local officials shape the experiences of immigrants after they arrive, focusing on integration rather than immigration decisions. They collaborate with local U.S. Citizenship and Immigration Services field offices for efficient decision-making. Local approaches to immigrant accommodation vary. New York City's "right to shelter" policy, for instance, provides housing regardless of legal status. Most places have no such right, leaving volunteer groups and immigrant groups to sort out housing issues.

Public schools must enroll immigrant children, but local policies dictate language of instruction and other types of support. While immigrant students have the right to education, they may not always receive native language instruction, often being placed in English-only programs. Local policies also extend to services like school lunch programs and how they are structured in ways that might or might not benefit immigrant children.

Despite immigration being federally governed, localities are immigrants' first points of contact. State and local governments also provide resources on their websites to guide immigrants and play a role in combatting immigration scams where newcomers may fall victim to fraudulent legal services. Public libraries sometimes establish "citizenship corners" or host immigration information sessions, offering newcomers the opportunity to learn about available resources.

Taxes

Federal Level

When your child starts working, they will most certainly wonder why their paycheck doesn't match their hourly wage. This can be your intro to talking about taxes. You know that taxes are collected by all government levels for public services, but for kids who start their first part-time job, the reality can be a harsh one. While they might not care about where their money goes, it's a good perspective builder to work through some of the details together.

Federal taxes are paid annually to the Internal Revenue Service (IRS). Payroll taxes, split between workers and employers, are collected with each pay period. Once the federal government collects tax revenue, it allocates it to various national interests. This includes funding the armed services, maintaining federal lands, managing borders and coastal waters, exploring space, supporting research and development, promoting the arts, law enforcement through the FBI, intelligence operations through the CIA, the overall functioning of the federal bureaucracy, and more. Congress can also appropriate funds for new programs or initiatives and provide grants to state and local governments to be used according to federal program guidelines. Payroll taxes specifically fund Medicare and Social Security, while other funds are more flexible and can be transferred across different government programs.

As to how this pertains to federalism, the federal government uses tax revenues for many purposes and does not have to distribute funds back to states equally. High-income states generally subsidize lower-income ones. Additionally, federal funds can be allocated to local governments for specific projects, such as updating government building systems for energy efficiency.

State Level

States have their own unique ways of collecting taxes and they have flexibility to do things around taxes that the federal government lacks. State governments can create things like temporary "tax holidays" for events like back-to-school shopping or emergency preparedness. States levy taxes on income, corporations, payroll, property, sales, and specific activities. Sales and property taxes are significant at these levels. Property taxes are based on home values and sales taxes added to purchases; these are two types of taxes that the federal government does not levy. State tax programs vary quite a bit. For example, New Jersey has the highest property tax rate, exceeding 2%, while Hawaii has the lowest at around 0.31%. Sales taxes are a percentage added to the purchase price of items within a jurisdiction. In Arizona, the state's base sales tax rate was 5.6% in 2022, but it can go as high as 11.2% in municipalities that also levy local taxes.

State and local taxes fund all sorts of different directed programs. Different items may have different tax rates, such as an additional "gas tax" on fuel purchases. Local sales taxes, known as Special Purpose Local Option Sales Taxes, can be applied to specific items like refinishing community pools or government building upgrades. Tax authorities, typically within the state treasury, oversee varying laws and incentives, like credits for energy-efficient home upgrades or hiring veterans.

State budgets tend to be spent mostly on public welfare, education, and healthcare, also covering infrastructure and community services.[6] For detailed state tax information where you live, consult your state government's online resources.

Local Level

Local governments fund their services mainly through property and sales taxes, but they also apply taxes to specific transactions like deed transfers and vehicle registrations. The tax structure varies with each locality's size, needs, and population. For example, bigger cities may have additional taxes to support public transportation systems. Local authorities often prioritize educational programs, economic incentives for businesses, infrastructure development, and public safety when determining how to use their budgets.

All levels of government have taxing authorities and levy taxes on individuals and businesses to fund public goods and services. The variations in tax policies from place to place can spark interesting discussions and questions for you and your child, particularly if they are curious about money, planning, and spending. Reviewing tax policies and comparing your area to others can be an eye-opening experience for both of you.

The Economy

Federal Level

Economic policy in federalism involves how government layers regulate and guide economic activity. Nearly everything that the federal government does has the capacity to influence the broader economy. Federal actions, like imposing new regulations, can shift economic resources, as compliance requires businesses and individuals to adapt.

One of the core powers reserved to the federal government in our federalist system is the ability to regulate interstate commerce. Because of this, federal economic policy can be targeted at job growth, prioritizing domestic production of things, or creating workplace policies to promote equity and fairness in hiring.

Another way the federal government plays a role in economic federalism is through intergovernmental grants. Federally passed appropriations bills can support regional, state, or local innovation ecosystems by providing funding for technological advancements and job creation, but these programs generally allow states or localities to determine how to use the funds. Thinking about the cooperative relationship between states and local governments is sometimes a better way to discuss federalism with your children. For instance, in many cases, you can visit local businesses and talk to people about how government works (or doesn't) to achieve their economic goals.

State Level

State-level economic policies play an important role in shaping the economic landscape of each state—and oftentimes surrounding states as well. Each state supports businesses with resources like Small Business Administrations, offering compliance assistance and state contracting guidance to foster economic growth.

Economic dynamics vary by state based on key industries. For example, Virginia heavily relies on defense spending, with 19% of its economy coming from this sector—the highest proportion among all states.[7] In tourist-rich states like Hawaii, legislation focuses more on conservation to support tourism. Florida's policies favor the citrus industry, with tax incentives and climate change measures to protect crops. These initiatives aim to benefit both the state's economy and the large number of constituents employed in these industries.

State governments often face the challenge of balancing competing economic incentives from different industries. For instance, in Maine, there are valuable lobster management areas dedicated to lobster growth, while offshore wind and oil developers may also seek access to these locations. State legislators must determine how to allocate the use of these natural resources, making decisions about who can and cannot utilize specific parts of the ocean. In the realm of sea and ocean regulations, federalism plays a role, as the federal government generally oversees the usage of oceans. However, in cases like the example from Maine, state officials have significant influence over activities in waters adjacent to their land, resulting in overlapping considerations and decision-making authority.

For working teens, understanding minimum wage differences is a practical federalism lesson. Some states have raised wages above the federal level, while others have not, reflecting federalism's ability to accommodate state-led initiatives. Conversations about minimum wage can link policy to teens' lives, showing how state decisions affect jobs and living costs. It's an opportunity to think about the effects of state-set wages on the economic landscape they're soon to enter.

Local Level

Local governments play a critical economic policy role due to their community connection. They most quickly address local needs, directly funding projects that enhance their area, especially post-disaster recovery efforts when crises strike.

When it comes to things like housing and transportation—which are all closely related to the economics of an area, decisions made at the local level have a lot of influence. Local governments best understand the distinct needs and aspirations of their communities, enabling them to tailor policies that promote local growth and opportunity. From zoning regulations that determine where businesses can operate to tax incentives that attract investment, local governments have a direct impact on job creation, infrastructure development, and overall economic vitality.

When you see new buildings going up or notice how smoothly traffic flows—or when you notice buildings falling into disrepair or intersections that seemed dangerous to drive through—all these choices are likely related to local government activity.

Take a drive or walk through your town and see if you can find things together with your children and think about how governments might approach making decisions to improve the public spaces of your area.

Fiscal federalism is really about divvying up responsibilities, both financial and administrative, among federal, state, and local governments. It's like piecing together a puzzle to make the economy run smoother and achieve public goals—but it's a puzzle that no two people generally agree on, and everyone feels like they are competing rather than working together—that's politics!

Healthcare Policy

Federal Level

Healthcare is another area where federalism is on display. The Affordable Care Act (ACA), also known as Obamacare, was a prime example of the federal government implementing policy changes at the top level that would, in turn, influence how state and local governments reacted in the healthcare space. This legislation mandated the creation of health insurance marketplaces, prevented insurance companies from denying coverage based on pre-existing conditions, expanded the eligibility criteria for Medicaid, and much more. Health insurance regulations have "teeth" precisely because of the federal government's role in overseeing the industry at a national level through their power to make policies that deal with interstate commerce.

Some other parts of healthcare policy, like Medicare and Medicaid, are first set up by the federal government, but states must still make their own policies for implementation. Medicare, which serves elderly individuals, provides essential health insurance to this demographic, while Medicaid extends coverage to low-income individuals and families. In this capacity, the federal government sets forth basic guidelines, allocates funding, and establishes regulations to govern the functioning of these programs, thereby influencing the healthcare landscape on a national level. But states determine eligibility requirements and are free to create their own policies around who must provide care, and how to do so for people within such programs.

State Level

A not-so-distant memory for most readers will be the COVID-19 pandemic. During that time, governments at all levels scrambled to figure out what their healthcare policies were going to be. The federal level took the lead on vaccine development, but each state was responsible for developing and implementing a vaccine distribution plan to meet the targeted needs of prioritized population groups. This is how a lot of health policy happens, with big provisions created by the federal government, and lots of details and administration happening at the state and local levels.

State governments have significant authority in shaping and regulating healthcare within their respective jurisdictions. For instance, states can establish and operate their own health insurance marketplaces or partner with the federal government's marketplace, and they have authority over regulating health insurance providers operating within their borders on rules related to coverage, premiums, network adequacy, and consumer protections.

States also have healthcare policy powers that are nearly exclusively theirs and don't involve much oversight from the federal government. State governments regulate healthcare professionals' licensing, including physicians, nurses, pharmacists, and other healthcare practitioners. They establish standards and requirements for education, training, and ongoing competency of healthcare professionals. State health departments also enforce regulations for healthcare facilities, such as hospitals and clinics.

Finally, state governments are also responsible for collecting and analyzing health data, such as vital statistics, disease prevalence, and healthcare utilization. They maintain systems for reporting and monitoring health information to track population health trends and inform policy decisions.

Local Level

The local level of government—counties, cities, and municipalities—plays a necessary role in healthcare, even if their authority isn't as extensive as that of federal and state governments. While they don't wield as much power as federal or state levels, their impact on community health policies and initiatives is significant.

Local bodies manage key public health services, such as restaurant health inspections, environmental hazard monitoring, and community health education. They also set local health regulations, which is why policies like the adoption of indoor smoking bans varied by area, as different localities decided where smoking would and would not be permitted.

Additionally, local authorities typically oversee emergency medical services, including ambulance operations and paramedic responses—often supported by local volunteers. Although they might receive federal or state grants, the responsibility for staffing, training, and maintaining these services lies with local government.

Environmental Policy

Federal Level

The federal government plays a key role in environmental policy, regulating air, water, and land use. Nature, however, doesn't recognize our administrative boundaries, necessitating a collaborative approach to environmental federalism.

At the national level, the government sets emission standards for various sectors and controls pollutants. The National Environmental Policy Act of 1970 mandates environmental impact assessments for significant projects. The Clean Water Act outlines water quality standards and pollution control, while the Resource Conservation and Recovery Act handles hazardous waste management. Central to many environmental policy goals is an agency you've probably heard of—the Environmental Protection Agency (EPA). Established in 1970 under President Richard Nixon's guidance, the EPA's mission is safeguarding both the environment and human health. This agency spearheads rule-setting and policy implementation on the national stage.

The federal reach extends to public land management through the U.S. Forest Service, National Park Service, and Bureau of Land Management, overseeing resource extraction and conservation. Something of interest to many kids is the protection of animals. At the federal level, we have the Endangered Species Act focusing on the protection and recovery of vulnerable species and their habitats as an example of a federal act toward the environment.

While broad nationally applicable policies are indeed a federal responsibility, environmental federalism must be factored into decisions made within state borders on federal lands.

State Level

States adopt different approaches to environmental policies, adapting their strategies to suit their distinct needs. Some states have Departments of Natural Resources, some call these the Department of Environment and Natural Resources, the Department of Environmental Health, the Department of Environmental Quality, and so on. Whatever the name, these state level agencies function as localized counterparts to the

EPA, addressing the specific environmental challenges within their state borders.

The uniqueness of each state's ecosystem necessitates state-specific policies. States rich in natural resources may favor different energy solutions like solar, wind, or fossil fuels, often setting their own renewable energy targets beyond federal mandates.

States and local governments—more than the federal government—are responsible for environmental policies around recycling and composting programs. Some states have ambitious recycling goals and implement programs to reduce landfill waste and promote sustainable waste management practices—others delegate much of that power to smaller local governments.

Offshore drilling illustrates federalism's complexity in environmental policy. Federal agencies manage seabed leasing and drilling, yet states advocate for their interests, considering the impact on local industries and economies. In places like South Carolina, where ocean industries like fisheries and tourism support approximately 32,000 jobs and generate over $2 billion in economic activity annually, state officials must weigh the benefits of drilling against the value of existing coastal economies, often influencing federal decisions and highlighting the interplay between federal and state governance.[8]

Local Level

Local environmental concerns hold immense importance for enhancing the quality of life within cities and towns. Decision-making processes surrounding zoning, safe drinking water, invasive species control, and disaster response are primarily conducted at the local level.

Zoning regulations at the local level hold environmental significance as they determine land usage and allocation. Open lands for public enjoyment, commercial lands for crop production, and wildlife habitats are each designated through zoning. Moreover, zoning laws can promote the creation of green spaces, parks, and community gardens in urban environments, enriching residents' environmental experiences.

While the federal government bears the basic responsibility of ensuring equitable access to safe drinking water, local water departments are instrumental in executing this task. An example of environmental federalism can been seen in Oregon, a state known for its natural beauty but grappling with many highly polluted waterways.[9] While the statewide Oregon Health Authority ensures public water systems comply with federal Safe Drinking Water Act standards, local and regional governments are tasked with the hands-on water planning and management.[10]

Invasive species control is another collaborative endeavor between local and state governments. Pennsylvania, for instance, established an Invasive Species Council in 2017 comprising local advisors across different parts of the state who identify and work to counteract harmful invasive species. This body is concerned with what happens in Pennsylvania, despite the fact that the state borders six other states.[11] If you're looking to address an environmental concern, your local representative is often the best starting point for involvement.

In disaster recovery, local governments are the first to respond. While federal and state support is necessary in the aftermath of large storms or catastrophes, local officials are the ones who coordinate the immediate response. As natural disasters become more and more common, some states have taken to hosting disaster response exercises as a way to better prepare and train local government officials about what to do when extreme weather threatens their cities and towns.[12] For parents with older teens, finding out how to prepare to effectively volunteer in such a situation can be a good way to understand local government in action and give back to your community.

Social Policies

Social policy is a broad and complex aspect of politics, covering issues from reproductive and abortion policies, to LGBTQ+ rights and public assistance programs, to much more. It relates to the governance of how we coexist within society's agreed-upon structures. For example, the 1973 *Roe v. Wade* decision once set a nationwide precedent for abortion policy. However, the landscape shifted dramatically with the 2022 *Dobbs v. Jackson Women's Health* decision, which enhanced states' authority in determining reproductive laws. While social policy areas are vast and ever-changing, recognizing the roles different government levels play can help demystify the topics that interest your children.

Federal Level

At the federal level, civil rights legislation forms the core of social policy. Key laws, like the Civil Rights Act of 1964 and the Americans with Disabilities Act of 1990, were enacted to guarantee equal rights for everyone, irrespective of their race, color, religion, sex, origin, or abilities. Such laws have wide-ranging implications. For example, Title VI of the Civil Rights Act bars discrimination in any program receiving federal funds, impacting various sectors including education and healthcare.

In a way that may be more immediately applicable to your children, Title IX of the Education Amendments of 1972 prohibits sex-based discrimination in educational programs and activities that receive federal funding. It covers educational institutions at all levels, from K–12 schools to colleges and universities. Title IX ensures that individuals are not denied access to educational opportunities based on their sex.

Beyond laws, different federal entities are responsible for the promulgation and enforcement of antidiscrimination efforts. The federal Equal Employment Opportunity Commission is responsible for enforcing federal laws that prohibit workplace discrimination. The commission is tasked with investigating complaints of discrimination in employment practices, such as hiring, promotion, and workplace treatment, and takes legal action against employers found to be engaging in discriminatory behavior based on any protected characteristic.

Social policies are some of the most hotly debated policies in the American political scene. However, changing these sorts of policies is quite difficult given the threshold necessary to move legislation forward in the House and the Senate. In recent times, much of this work on what we consider social policy has taken place within the states.

State Level

Social policies at the state level encompass more than addressing discrimination; they often involve distributing benefits to individuals. Commonly known as welfare or public assistance, these policies are designed to ensure a basic quality of life for all U.S. residents. One of the most well-known programs is the Temporary Assistance for Needy Families (TANF) program, a federal program with state-level implementation. TANF aims to provide assistance to families so that children may be cared for in their own homes or in the homes of relatives, while also promoting job readiness for parents who are dependent on the government for financial assistance. The responsibility for implementing these programs primarily rests with the states, which have the authority to determine eligibility criteria, benefit amounts, and program requirements.

Another focal point in current social policy discussions is access to reproductive healthcare, including preventative medical interventions and abortion services. Following the 1973 *Roe v. Wade* decision, states initially had a minimum provision allowing women to seek abortion access up to 24 weeks of pregnancy. However, this issue has now shifted to the states, with each taking their own approach. The federal government also lacks a provision guaranteeing women and young girls access to reliable birth control or establishing uniform sex education programs for all children. Instead, states utilize a variety of policy mechanisms to determine their own policies.

State provisions for abortion access are all over the map. Recently introduced legislation in a number of states could ban most abortions, except in cases of maternal health, rape, or incest that have been reported to law enforcement. This potential ban has prompted challenges from Planned Parenthood and other providers, who argue it violates individuals' rights. Meanwhile, Texas saw a December 2023 case where a woman, pregnant with a terminally ill fetus, was granted and then denied the right to an abortion by differing court decisions, with the state's attorney general expressing intentions to prosecute any physician who performs the procedure in such circumstances.[13] The landscape on abortion policy is solidly in the hands of the states now, in a way that we haven't known for nearly 50 years.

Local Level

At the local level, social policy decisions can significantly shape the everyday quality of life within a community. Consider libraries, recreation centers, and community hubs—they all serve as pivotal points of connection in a community's social fabric. Also at this level, services like Child Protective Services and Domestic Violence Prevention are necessary for protecting the most vulnerable among us, ensuring safety for children and those in abusive situations.

Social challenges vary by community, each with its own distinct needs. If you're looking to make an impact, consider joining local organizations already addressing these issues. Drawing inspiration from various local programs can be a springboard for initiating change in your own community in a way that you want to see change.

Infrastructure Policy

Federal Level

Infrastructure is a broad concept. The federal government funds and regulates significant infrastructure, covering transportation, energy, waterways, and communications, particularly for projects extending across state lines. Federal agencies like the Federal Highway Administration and the Federal Aviation Administration manage interstate infrastructure, including highways and airports. Multiple levels of government support energy grid maintenance and renewable projects. Energy pipelines such as the proposed Keystone XL pipeline are under the control of the federal government, though the starts and stops of this project are largely dictated by which political party wields control in the capital with Democrats stressing the need to move away from legacy fuels and Republicans arguing for an all-styles-possible approach to energy policy.

In a way that infrastructure overlaps with national defense, the U.S. Space Command protects satellite systems necessary for the military, but also used for GPS and communication technology by people all over the United States.

The Federal Communications Commission regulates communications infrastructure, with a focus on reducing the digital divide. Nearly a quarter of rural Americans lack broadband, which is critical for services like banking and healthcare.[14] To address this, the federal Affordable Connectivity Program helps eligible households with internet costs and subsidizes computer purchases.[15] State and local government also have policies to deal with internet infrastructure, but the federal government can spend more money on this issue—as is true for nearly everything else.

State Level

Many of the infrastructure matters we encounter in our daily lives are within the realm of state governance. State governments take charge of constructing and maintaining local roads and highways, ensuring smooth transportation networks that cater to communities within their boundaries. The scope of these responsibilities is often substantial. Beyond managing networks of physical infrastructure, state leaders must also navigate the intricacies of federal laws that occasionally complicate their tasks. One issue that illustrates this challenge is the issue of logging truck collisions, which have been on the rise since 2011.[16] These wrecks often occur on city, county, or state roads due to a quirk in current federal law: logging trucks aren't permitted to use interstate highways. Federalism has pain points as well as upsides.

Public transit systems, such as buses, light-rail, and subways, are another infrastructure component under state jurisdiction. In this capacity, state legislators have the ability to set fare structures and determine service routes. While the iconic New York City subway system is associated with life in the Big Apple, it's the state of New York that largely manages these operations. The state level wields both the financial resources required to run the system and the authority to implement changes.

Like other areas, there is a good deal of federal and state cooperation in infrastructure policy. For example, the federal Infrastructure Investment and Jobs Act of 2021 was designed to help transit agencies replace aging rail rolling stock, to improve the reliability and safety of our country's rail transit systems. States in turn received different amounts of funding from the Federal Transit Authority's Rail Vehicle Replacement program—which they then may use to contract with local businesses to modernize their own vehicles in ways that the community determines to be important.

States also contribute to expanding broadband internet access, often administering federal funds through entities like a Broadband Development Authority. These state agencies prioritize community input in deciding the allocation and implementation of these funds.

Local Level

Local governments manage different sorts of infrastructure that affects our daily lives, such as water services, sewage, drainage, and water treatment. They also oversee transportation infrastructure including roads, bike paths, and public transit facilities, which not only allow us to get around but also help to drive economic growth. The synergy between local, state, and federal governments on infrastructure projects is visible on things like road maintenance where collaboration is required across finances, hiring, and maintenance efforts.

For road maintenance, agencies like the Federal Highway Administration offer funds that complement local budgets for infrastructure upkeep. State and local governments are responsible for contracting out or conducting the work necessary to keep things flowing smoothly for cars, bikes, and pedestrians. Recent federal legislation like the National Defense Authorization Act of 2021 and the Bipartisan Infrastructure Law of 2022 injected billions into transportation improvements. The American Rescue Plan of 2021 also supported local community enhancement. This legislation allocated significant funds for projects like the creation of new bike paths, connecting neighborhoods that previously lacked adequate options.

Have a look around your town and see what sorts of local infrastructure projects have developed in the past 10 years. If you can't seem to find any, have a call with your local government to discuss projects where you'd like to see improvement and you might just start the ball rolling in building a better community for you and your neighbors.

Public Safety and Policing

Federal Level

Public safety and policing provide a clear example of the intricate interplay of federalism. All government officials share the commitment to serve the American people, and a fundamental way this commitment materializes is by ensuring the safety of all individuals. At the federal level, specific law enforcement agencies have distinct roles in safeguarding our nation. Agencies like the FBI, the Drug Enforcement Administration (DEA), and the Bureau of Alcohol, Tobacco, Firearms and Explosives (ATF) operate nationally, addressing crimes that span state boundaries or have broader federal implications.

The FBI handles a broad spectrum of security issues from terrorism to cybercrime. The DEA adapts to the current drug landscape, currently focusing on a synthetic drug influx such as fentanyl, while the ATF regulates alcohol, tobacco, firearms, and explosives.

While states and localities often dictate police training and standards, the federal government can exert influence through funding incentives. Federal agencies can offer grants to law enforcement bodies that adhere to specific training and accreditation criteria, promoting the adoption of best practices. For instance, in 2023, Pennsylvania celebrated the allocation of $250,000 in federal funds to train 600 police officers in de-escalation techniques in Lackawanna County—this was a state level "victory" in getting funding for training, and a federal "victory" in promoting de-escalation tactics in policing.

State Level

State governments set law enforcement training and certification standards within their states, tailoring programs and procedures to their specific needs with no two states doing things the same way. Despite the power to set the training regulations, a significant portion of training procedures at the state level are influenced by federal priorities and are often bolstered by federal funding. For example, in 2023, state police departments had the opportunity to access federal funds designated by the U.S. Department of Justice for immersive virtual reality technology aimed at enhancing law enforcement training.[17] This is a similar de-escalation initiative to that mentioned above that used new technologies, including virtual reality systems to simulate scenarios and allow police to practice responses in ways that are de-escalatory in a manner that better serves law enforcement and people by reducing violence and fatalities.

States are responsible for defining their own criminal laws, from offenses and penalties to sentencing. State law enforcement, including state police and highway patrol, upholds these laws.

Federalism isn't solely about funding law enforcement priorities from the top down. It's a two-way relationship. State governments collaborate with federal agencies on various facets of law enforcement sharing information, pooling resources, and synching strategies in realms like drug enforcement, immigration control, and counterterrorism. Although states possess substantial authority in these domains, they must simultaneously uphold the federal constitutional safeguards and rights.

Local Level

The federal government takes an active role in bolstering local community policing efforts with funding and resources. One of the most expansive efforts in this vein is the Community Oriented Policing Services (COPS) program, an initiative that channels grants to support community engagement of local police organizations.

Beyond simple policing effectiveness, the reach of COPS funds extends to targeted endeavors like School Violence Prevention Programs as well. An illustration of this sort of effort can be found in the aftermath of the tragic events at Robb Elementary School in Uvalde, Texas, where a gunman took the lives of 17 children and two educators. The community received over $1 million to revamp their school violence prevention measures as an effort to protect against such violence in the future.

Local police departments operate at the municipal or county level while being subject to the regulatory oversight of state governments. State laws dictate the scope of authority and responsibilities of local law enforcement agencies. Like at the state level, the interaction is a two-way dynamic involving the flow of funds from federal and state programs, while also facilitating the transmission of support and valuable intelligence up the chain for ongoing investigations.

Education and Schools

Federal Level

Education and school policy are usually set by state and local actors. However, the federal government oversees the U.S. service academies, which includes the U.S. Naval Academy, U.S. Air Force Academy, U.S. Military Academy, and U.S. Merchant Marine Academy, and K–12 military schools.

Just as federal funding can shape policing, federal influence extends to education policy through funding and grants, affecting programs like those that offer support for disadvantaged students and teacher training. These funds often come with specific conditions and guidelines that states and school districts must follow to access the funding.

The federal Department of Education, the smallest among all federal departments, reflects the balance of power for states and localities in education matters. While acknowledging that local authorities have the ultimate say in most educational decisions, federal legislators still allocate budgets that enhance school funding through federal backing. In the fiscal year 2023 federal budget bill, $45 billion was designated for education, a $3.2 billion increase from the previous budget. These funds are intended for K–12 education programs, aimed at ensuring quality and equitable education, supporting students with special needs, and expanding mental health resources in schools.

Federal legislation, particularly the Every Student Succeeds Act (ESSA), mandates states to implement standardized testing to assess student performance in core subjects. ESSA also enforces accountability measures, specifying how schools should be evaluated based on test outcomes, graduation rates, and other benchmarks. In addition, ESSA allocates funds for school districts to acquire tech tools like iPads and robots, meant to provide learning experiences in coding, math, and problem-solving.

In higher education, the federal government plays a role by offering financial aid programs such as Pell Grants, Direct Loans, and work-study opportunities. Each year, nearly six million students pursue higher education through the assistance of Pell Grants.[18] Another significant support avenue is Federal Work-Study (FWS), a program administered by higher education institutions, providing students with paid work and research opportunities beyond the classroom. This book was made possible through the collaborative efforts of five FWS research assistants.

Federal policies also address issues like fairness in school funding and the nutritional content of school lunches. However, most determinations—like school start and end times, activity offerings, and appropriate classroom instruction—are generally made at the state and local levels. This form of "hands-off federalism" contributes to the varied nature of civic education across the United States. There's no federal standard for teaching civics. Each high school, district, or state sets its own educational guidelines regarding what students should know upon graduation. This is one of the key reasons it is up to us as parents to make sure our children know how to wield their power when they are old enough to do so.

State Level

State education departments, collaborating with legislators and governors, address statewide educational issues, from teacher certification to school session lengths and meal policies, including decisions on school closures when necessary. Curriculum and content standards for K–12 education are set by state policymakers, determining subjects, content, and student skill targets. Some states make decisions even about the textbooks and instructional materials used in their classrooms—though many allocate these decisions to smaller, local bodies.

Teacher certification standards are state-specific, involving educational prerequisites and exams. Union negotiations often involve state-level discussions, shaping teacher conditions and contracts. The largest share of funding responsibility for education falls squarely on states' shoulders, despite the existence of federal funding programs. States oversee the allocation of funds to various school districts, which in turn shapes the resources available for teachers, school infrastructure, and program equity across a state.

State level debates around permissible teaching content often revolve around topics like sex education, gender and sexuality, evolution, and the portrayal of historical events and figures, reflecting the varied concerns of parents within a community. Decisions made at the state level can greatly influence the education landscape, emphasizing the importance of community engagement in shaping educational policies. If you have something that feels problematic at your school, it might take going to the state level to solve it.

Local Level

Local school districts, guided by state standards, tailor the curriculum to their community's needs. They decide on teaching methods, materials, and lesson plans. Local school districts and even schools themselves are responsible for recruiting, hiring, and evaluating teachers and staff. Everything from teacher contracts to salaries and professional development opportunities comes under their purview. Superintendents—the executives of school systems—are typically appointed by school boards and are responsible for setting district priorities.

Local governments shape daily school operations, including schedules, class sizes, extracurricular activities, and facility upgrades. This also means that they oversee how instruction is delivered to students. For example, during the COVID-19 pandemic, district-level decisions were those that determined if students were in virtual, hybrid, or in-person learning models.

School districts operate with autonomy but within the bounds of state and federal laws. Education, unlike other political issues, is primarily managed at the local level and offers a platform for parents and students to effect change. This means that in some ways, changing parts of education policy are the easiest sorts of changes for parents or students to influence. As you and your children talk about politics, see if you think having school programming that dealt with the topic would be possible. You can talk to other parents or have the kids themselves propose changes to the school. Change favors those who advocate, so if you think this is a topic that would be beneficial to cover in schools, consider your possible routes to political action to make that so.

Federalism as an Evolving Principle

Federalism in the United States today is far from what the country's founders envisioned over two centuries ago. The Constitution made for federal and state government partnership, sketching the boundaries of their spheres, but it also left many governmental roles and responsibilities ambiguous. In the ensuing years, the roles of federal, state, and local governments have continually shifted, adapting to different circumstances and public opinion.

In the twenty-first century, the government landscape has transformed, with the federal, state, and local sectors expanding their reach in their own ways, and ceding power in other ways. The federal and state governments are the primary sources of funding for public expenditures, while the influence of local governments has waned. Over time, the federal government has expanded its role in domains traditionally entrusted to state and local governments. One example is the Affordable Care Act (ACA), enacted in 2010. While healthcare has traditionally been under state regulation, the ACA established federal standards for healthcare insurance, expanding coverage, and mandating individuals to have health insurance. In a parallel move, state governments have also broadened their jurisdiction into areas that were once the exclusive terrain of local governments. Historically, zoning laws and decisions about land use have been the prerogative of municipalities and counties. In California, for instance, the state has passed laws that limit the ability of local governments to block the development of new housing.

Reflecting these shifts in the federalist landscape, the volume of intergovernmental grants—often in the form of categorical or special-purpose grants—flowing from higher to lower levels of government has expanded across many policy spaces.

The specific policies governed under federalism constantly evolve. Yet, the principles that allocate different governmental responsibilities to distinct levels remain. Understanding these principles offers a roadmap to comprehending the inner workings of government and policy. As various issues pique your or your kids' interest, recognizing which level of government holds the power is your first step to making a difference. By understanding a little bit of intricacy, you can paint a picture that political decision-making isn't a monolithic process confined to the corridors of Washington DC. Instead, it's done by numerous local and state players, shaping decisions that significantly influence our day-to-day lives.

Online Resources for State Government:

National Governors Association www.nga.org.

Council of State Governments www.csg.org.

USA.Gov (Contact Information for Each State/Territory) https://www.usa.gov/states-and-territories.

National Conference of State Legislatures www.ncsl.org.

Library of Congress State Government Information https://www.loc.gov/rr/news/stategov/index.html.

State and Local Government on the Net www.statelocalgov.net/.

Federal and State Constitutions, Statutes, and Codes https://www.law.cornell.edu/statutes.

Online Resources for Local Government:

National League of Cities www.nlc.org.

National Association of Counties www.naco.org.

USA.Gov (Contact Information for Local Governments, by State) https://www.usa.gov/local-governments.

Notes

1. U.S. Census Bureau. (2019). 2019 American Community Survey 1-Year Estimates.
2. Exec. Order No. 13767, 82 Fed. Reg. 8793 (2017).
3. Rosenberg, E. (2017). Federal judge blocks Trump's executive order on denying funding to sanctuary cities. *The Washington Post* (21 November). https://www.washingtonpost.com/news/politics/wp/2017/11/21/federal-judge-blocks-trumps-executive-order-on-denying-funding-to-sanctuary-cities/.

4. U.S. Department of Homeland Security. (2022). President Biden to announce uniting for Ukraine, a new streamlined process to welcome Ukrainians fleeing Russia's invasion of Ukraine. Press release (21 April). https://www.dhs.gov/news/2022/04/21/president-biden-announce-uniting-ukraine-new-streamlined-process-welcome-ukrainians.

5. Immigration Legal Resource Center. (n.d.). www.ilrc.org.

6. U.S. Census Bureau. (2020). Annual survey of state and local government finances, 1977–2020.

7. U.S. Department of Defense. (2021). 2021 readiness and environmental protection integration program. State Fact Sheets | Virginia. https://www.repi.mil/Portals/44/Documents/State_Fact_Sheets/Virginia_StateFacts.pdf.

8. South Carolina Department of Natural Resources. (2017). The economic contribution of natural resources to South Carolina's economy.

9. Oregon has the dubious distinction of having the greatest number of its waterways classified as "impaired," affecting aquatic life, drinking water, and recreation. Kelderman, K., Phillips, A., Pelton, T., et al. (2022). The Clean Water Act at 50: Promises half kept at the half-century mark. Environmental Integrity Project (17 March). https://environmentalintegrity.org/wp-content/uploads/2022/03/CWA@50-report-3-17-22.pdf.

10. Samayoa, M. (2022). Groundwater pollution puts drinking water at risk in Eastern Oregon counties. OPB (5 May). https://www.opb.org/article/2022/05/05/groundwater-pollution-eastern-oregon-counties-drinking-water-at-risk-farming-wells/.

11. The Governor's Invasive Species Council. (n.d.). About us. Pennsylvania Department of Agriculture. https://www.agriculture.pa.gov/Plants_Land_Water/PlantIndustry/GISC/Pages/About-Us.aspx.

12. The Texas A&M University. (2023). Texas prepares for hurricane season with full-scale hurricane exercise (18 May).

13. Goodman, D. (2023). Texas Supreme Court temporarily halts court-approved abortion. *The New York Times* (8 December). https://www.nytimes.com/2023/12/08/us/texas-abortion-court-ken-paxton.html.

14. Wireline Competition. (2012). Eighth broadband progress report. Federal Communications Commission (21 August). https://www.fcc.gov/reports-research/reports/broadband-progress-reports/eighth-broadband-progress-report#:~:text=In%20rural%20areas%2C%20nearly%20one,Americans%20still%20do%20not%20subscribe.

15. Institute for Local Self Reliance. (n.d.). Affordable connectivity program dashboard. https://acpdashboard.com/.

16. Cole, N.B., Barrett, S.M., Bolding, M.C., and Aust, W.M. (2019). An analysis of fatal log truck crashes in the United States from 2011 through 2015. *International Journal of Forest Engineering* 30(2): 121–131.

17. Bureau of Justice Assistance. (2023). FY 2023 virtual reality de-escalation site-based initiative. U.S. Department of Justice. https://bja.ojp.gov/funding/opportunities/o-bja-2023-171767.

18. National Center for Educational Statistics. (n.d.). Financial aid: What is the percent of undergraduate students awarded Pell Grants? Institute of Education Sciences. https://nces.ed.gov/ipeds/trendgenerator/app/answer/8/35.

CHAPTER
9

Where to Go from Here

Our country is politically divided, and that's beyond the control of any one family. But as families, we can control how we communicate with and listen to one another. We can control the prioritization of civic know-how. And importantly, we are responsible for raising the next generation of citizens, so we can do more to teach our kids about politics and government.

Democracy relies on the exchange of information and ideas, with everyone having an opportunity to participate. However, in conversations about politics and government, it often feels like people are talking *at* each other rather than engaging in genuine discussion *with* each other. This poses a problem for our society. The success of our democratic experiment hinges on trust and understanding, which serve as the foundations of government legitimacy and community cohesion. When we don't know the basics, it's hard to have reasonable conversations. When we demonize politicians and government instead of seeking more information, we perpetuate a problem. When we are unable to express our views and truly listen to others, our understanding of shared problems suffers, and we miss out on opportunities to find solutions. Just like in sports or teamwork at school or work, we are more likely to succeed when we engage in discussions, work together, and seek common ground.

A child's political experiences, knowledge, and future behavior are shaped by their environment. This includes their school, friends, media exposure, socioeconomic and ethnic backgrounds, and, most importantly, their home and family life.[1] By avoiding discussions about politics and government with our children, we leave them ill-prepared to navigate the realities of our world. We cannot expect them to suddenly become all knowing, agents of change when they become eligible to vote. Schools have a hard time carving out curricular time for civics, and teachers are reticent to talk about politics. This means that many kids will not have practice in having political discussions or exercising political power unless we as parents decide to do something.

The role of a parent has one fundamental deliverable: to raise a self-sufficient individual capable of functioning in society. As parents, we all share the goal of supporting our children as they transition into adulthood. At its core, raising children is creating the next version of society. We should help our children develop a sense of self-efficacy—a feeling that they can do something to change an element of their world. Political self-efficacy is all but impossible to harness if you don't understand how the system operates. In the same way we teach children how to pack their own lunch or teach teens how to make appointments to see a doctor, lessons about the "how to" of government and politics help the next generation realize and use their own power.

In the same way you can pass down music appreciation or a love of sport, you can pass down the value of understanding your government. We as parents are all subjects of the political system; we owe it to our kids to make sure they understand that system as they become capable of fully participating in it.

Engaging in politics doesn't mean that we all have to be consumed by it, but having a working knowledge of how things function and being open to discussing those topics with our children benefit us all.

Our children have more than a lifetime of problems to sort out, many of which we are responsible for creating. It is not my hope that you talk to your children so that they can clean up our messes. It is my hope that by talking to our children, we can usher in a better, more caring, and more thoughtful system of politics . . . and as a side effect, some of our mistakes will be remedied by their efforts. In the same way we have fond memories of our parents cooking with us or teaching us a new sport, having a generation of children who grow up with memories of how their parents participated in politics and involved them in the process would go a long way in normalizing political discussions and rearing a set of more politically effective citizens. The children and young adults I see today are hopeful and full of heart, they want a better future, and we can help them along by being more willing to have hard conversations.

A commitment to the education of future generations allows for the development of leaders who can make reasoned decisions and can help our country better itself domestically and globally by having more peaceful disagreements at home and being a model to the world at large.

The United States is severely lacking in civic education. Schools focus so intensely on creating good test takers and boosting standardized test scores that they fail to create well-informed citizens. In school systems that are hyper-focused on memorizing and regurgitating facts, there is not a ton of room for learning and thinking about civics. Civics and politics are not mere tasks to be solved; they are processes to be understood, challenged, and changed. These topics require repeated discussions and continued emphasis as a child encounters new parts of life. Though math, reading comprehension, and science are more readily assessed by homework, quizzes, and standardized tests, the examination of civic knowledge persists throughout our entire lifetimes.

Do not fear that this work will be boring—it won't. Children love to feel like grown-ups. Think about the pride on a small child's face when they first tie their shoes, or better yet when they help a younger child master the skill. No matter how mundane a task or topic may seem to you, children love to gather more knowledge and act with their new skills. Don't expect perfection or absolute retention of all the things you talk about, but start building a vocabulary of politics and government with your children. And there is no need to make this feel like a chore or to belabor specific points. Let them know how they can participate and contribute, and they will start to develop competence in the subject. More importantly, they'll develop confidence in holding discussions of their own, advocating for their own opinions, and with practice, learn to listen and understand others.

When your children are in high school, discussions about politics and government can also help them develop ideas about their own values. Considering how political topics have multiple perspectives allows older children to try on different approaches and see what works best for them. This sort of practice also allows them to anticipate the sorts of things they'll want to get involved with when they leave the family home.

Family dinners are a great place to have these talks. But so are car rides, days at the beach, walks around your city, and hiking trips. In fact, many of the educators I talked to stressed that talking to teens in a setting when you're not looking face-to-face at them is a better way to connect with them, so take advantage of your car or walk time.

Setting an open and welcoming environment on these topics allows you to keep the conversations going with your child. Talking about current events as they happen allows each member of your family to develop a richer understanding about issues as they unfold. It enhances the critical thinking capacity of every family member when they can think about pressing topics in real and interesting ways. Children are naturally hungry to know more about the world around them, and when you show that you too are willing to learn alongside them, you are working to create a more thoughtful citizen. Of course, you get to decide what topics are appropriate for your family and which sorts of conversations you are willing to have. But lifting the taboo on politics and allowing some positive ideas about government into the mix means that we may very well get a set of young citizens who are more hopeful about their abilities to think and solve many of our important collective issues.

If you don't know where to start with your children, brainstorm with another adult, maybe your spouse or a good friend, about issues where you can see and appreciate different perspectives. Be willing to seek out information. Try to get as good a grasp as you can on the processes and players that are necessary to act on the issues you decide to talk about. And if your child wishes to act or advocate for some sort of change, be willing to hear them out and offer support if you can. City councils and local school boards are more than welcoming to precocious youngsters who have things to say. And if your child just wants to talk with you, have that conversation and allow that to be the sort of learning it can be on its own.

Our children remember the things we do and *don't* do. I remember my mom being willing to do crafts with me, but I never remember her talking about government with me or showing me how to exercise. I entered adulthood fully ready to use a glue gun and with a healthy appreciation for glitter, but I hardly knew anything about government and couldn't tell a barbell from a dumbbell. You don't have to be a parent who talks about politics around the clock, but don't let your children remember you as someone who never engaged the subject with them. We can all learn from our parents and improve upon things that we wish were in place when we were younger. After all, part of living a fulfilling adult life is realizing your own political power, and imparting bits and pieces of that experience to your children is worthwhile.

Ask your children what they've heard, what they think, what they know and what they want to know more about. Chances are, they'll be able to open your eyes to topics they have questions about, and you'll get to follow their lead. Ask them questions from a place of kindness as an attempt to better understand their positions, rather than working to persuade them to adopt yours. Ask them to think through the consequences of any changes they'd like to propose. And remember to thank them for having the courage to talk with you about the parts of government they don't understand and especially the parts of politics that they see differently than you do.

A lot of these lessons about politics and government transmitted from parents to children will be caught, not taught. Our children are thirsty mental sponges who try to make sense of the world in everything they do. But it is undeniable that our effort matters to our children. The way we approach these topics, and the sorts of engagements we are willing to have, shows our children how to consider politics and political discussions in the future.

Beyond talking, make sure to model the behavior that you think will help them. Take them to vote with you. Take them to government meetings. Let them meet your city council member. Encourage them to write to a member of government that they admire or disagree with.

And some lessons will be neither taught nor caught, but instead your children will learn on their own with your encouragement. For instance, on the issue of partisanship, I've stressed that the point is not to raise little Democrats or Republicans, but rather to raise politically autonomous children who know how to stay curious about government and where to look when they've got questions. You simply can't dictate this part to your kids. Besides, no one wins if we try to push our children toward a party that doesn't resonate with their own internal sense of political values. If your kids come to you asking about political parties, you are of course welcome to tell them which party (if any) you prefer. But for them to figure out what *they* prefer you can point them toward the official party platforms, which are typically revised every four years in anticipation of the presidential election. You can point them to the party leaders at the national level. Or better yet, you can figure out what local party organizations are in operation near you and help them attend a meeting.

By letting them figure things out about partisanship on their own, you are showing them how to think for themselves rather than relying on you or others to make up their minds for them.

Political identity is not just about who you vote for, but it's about what you value, what issues matter the most to you, and who you want to associate with and work alongside in the goal of creating a better country. One party is not better than the other, they are just different, so letting your kids try out a few identities is something that can be beneficial for kids. What's better is partisan identity is switchable, so be open to letting your children—and yourself—change.

If your children don't turn out like you in a partisan sense, that is not a failure. This can be hard for some of us to swallow, especially those who hold their political identity as a core identity. But our children see the world differently, they will navigate different challenges, they will think of new ideas, the parties will change, and party identity is only one way of communicating who they are and how they plan to do that.

In some ways, raising a child in a home that openly discusses politics to such a degree that extreme disagreement is permitted, and as a result, your child comes to a different conclusion than you did for the big question of partisanship, is actually a marker of success. You'll love your children anyhow and be that much more of an example to your community at large on how to both agree and disagree on different parts of life. In this hyper-partisan moment, being open to different viewpoints is a gift.

Raising children means imparting skills such as being on time, how to get dressed, how to pack an overnight bag for the weekend. We focus on developing strong math grades, piano talent, or competitive sports skills. And sometimes these take over in preparing kids for college. But it doesn't have to trade off with preparing kids to become participating citizens. Unlike sporting events that have winners and losers or music and dance recitals, politics and government are more of a process than an event. Sure, there are elections and protests and town hall meetings and bill signings, but to ensure your child appreciates their full power, make sure they know and understand the process. Start small and local, since the processes that happen at these levels are more immediate than national politics.

Talking about politics and government does not have to be difficult. Even if you find it challenging, take a minute to think about all the difficult topics many other people must discuss with their children as a matter of course: people in the process of immigrating, those who find themselves reliant on government nutrition services, people with loved ones serving in the U.S. military. All these families *must* care about and understand different features of government and policy. It is only fair that the rest of us show up and make sure we are invested and involved as well. This will take practice, but with repeated attempts and with more and more parents taking up the topic with children, we really can have a better political environment.

There has been a renewed interest in raising resilient children, children who are taught it's okay to fail, and that adversity is a part of life, but that the important thing is to know how to get back up and try again. Teaching your children about politics gives them a valuable set of tools that can aid in developing resilience. Politics provides plenty of opportunities to feel both wins and losses. Knowing how this all happens allows children to be more resilient in understanding that things are ever changing, and politics can be influenced by us all.

This book is not meant to add to your stresses as a parent; rather, it's meant to remove one taboo and equip you to talk more freely with your kids. Don't feel like you need to know everything about politics or government—just have an open mind to discussing these things with your children. By doing that, you are showing your children a valuable, social role adults play that they can someday pass on to the children in their lives. Doing this work may also spark a sense of greater purpose for your child, and having something to strive toward is generally related to increased happiness and satisfaction even when things don't work out as planned. Having your child interested in politics and government and equipped to think about big topics may inspire them to do more and allow them to chart a path that impacts people beyond themselves. I say this with great care, as I find too many young adults in college describing a sense of emptiness. Your child may not find the one true thing they care the most about during your family discussions, but having the opportunity to engage with great civic topics of our time means they will be more likely to find something that motivates them to do and be more for their communities.

You, too, may have to find a part about politics or government that you care about in order to model this behavior for your kids. But showing them that you care is a big deal. If you are coming at this task without a part of politics or government that is particularly interesting for you, maybe follow the lead of your children and try to learn more about an issue they care about. If they are interested because they feel like something is unjust or unfair, allow them to express that opinion and brainstorm ideas on how to be a part of change. If they care about something because it's an example of government doing something they like, foster that sense and encourage them to get more involved. Help them think through how they can be a part of the system, whether that is to get a better outcome or to ensure that something they like stays in place. Try to think back on what you were interested in at their age and share your failures or successes. And try to see and talk about the good parts of your experience caring about an issue, even if the outcome today is still not where you'd like it to be.

For me, an area of particular interest has been equal pay and equal treatment of women in the workplace. Though things are not fully equitable today, things are much better than they were when my mother had me, and much better than when her mother had her. In my own life, I've made it a point to know about who worked to improve the collective situation of women workers. I've also made it a point to live my politics, by speaking up in my own workplace and encouraging others to do the same. I have talked about this issue with my daughter since she was seven, and will continue to follow, participate in, teach on, and talk about the political and government happenings that influence equitable pay and treatment.

Politics in general and power specifically sometimes have negative connotations, but politics and power can also mean using one's voice to advocate for positive change. When thinking about different roles of government and talking through the strength of understanding and wielding power, make sure that your children know that it is theirs to harness. There is nothing negative about wanting to learn more and understand how our government operates. Children are curious and they want to grow. Part of this growth can be filled by a better understanding of how the world operates. There is nothing dirty or negative in learning about power and politics. All children want to find purpose and meaning as they mature; by allowing politics and government to be a topic of conversation from an early age, more children may be called to ponder some of our hardest questions and develop better solutions than what we have now.

Raising a child for them to be a successful adult does not just mean building a résumé. It means cultivating life skills to participate in public life. Think about skills related to politics and government as a matter of course, versus as a bonus. Help your children acquire these skills and you'll be allowing them to better function in the world as independent adults. One of the simplest ways to help is just to be available to have these conversations at all. What's more, we all stand to benefit from a generation of politically knowledgeable and engaged kids. People who find their passion at a young age tend to do some of their best work as young adults—they have time to ruminate on their ideas, think big, and get started toward excellence early. For the bigger problems that plague us like polarization, electoral reform, equity and justice, and the continued propagation of democracy, having a set of young, imaginative minds will surely do us good. Having a passion for government can spark a life's work of greatness.

In being a parent, you have been given the awesome task of raising a new generation. In being a teacher, I have had the humbling experience of seeing how all sorts of homes can produce political thinkers of all types. I close my semesters with the same message that I start with: politics is inevitable. Whether you choose to know about and use the system is up to you—but remember that the system will know about and use you, so you might as well understand as much as you can.

Thank you for reading this, thank you for your openness, and thank you for all the discussions you'll have with your children on this topic.

Note

1. De Landtsheer, C., Kalkhoven, L., Heirman, W., and De Vries, P. (2018). Talking politics at the dinner table: Stereotypes in children's political choices. *PCS–Politics, Culture and Socialization* 7(1+2): 19–20.

More Praise for *How to Raise a Citizen*

"Taking her philosophy on tough conversations from the classroom to the public, Lindsey Cormack's *How to Raise a Citizen* is an invaluable resource for understanding the importance of early civic engagement and provides all of the necessary tools to contextualize our democratic system for the next generation of voters."

—Madison Telles,
former student of Lindsey Cormack

"As edifying as it is urgent, *How to Raise a Citizen* is a service to parents interested in equipping their children for inevitable political realities and inspiring positive change in our system. In a time when defeatism, misinformation, and overwhelming negativity plague our system, we often need reminders of our agency to inspire change. *How to Raise a Citizen (And Why It's Up to You to Do It)* provides another such reminder while bringing new consideration to the duty parents hold in a child's civic upbringing."

— Brendan Mulligan,
University of Michigan Law School '27

"An essential primer on government and politics delivered in an engaging way. A must-read!"

—Dasha Yerokin,
former student of Lindsey Cormack from
Stevens Institute of Technology

"Professor Cormack's classes at Stevens University were the most educational hours of the week. She created an engaging and thought-provoking environment, fostering interest in our civil society and filling gaps in my understanding of the political system. With her book *How to Raise a Citizen*, she instills this same level of deep consideration and lively discussion, offering readers the tools they need to easily navigate our governmental system today."

—M.J.,
former student of Lindsey Cormack

"For parents and non-parents alike, *How to Raise a Citizen* outlines a blueprint for thoughtful, engaging, and productive conversations about politics and governance. Lindsey Cormack takes the complex issue of civic disengagement and offers digestible solutions to foster a future where political discussions can be less contentious."

—Conor Barren
former student of Lindsey Cormack

"Lindsey Cormack sparked my interest in politics as a college student with her ability to make politics fun and interesting for everyone. Now *How to Raise a Citizen* has inspired me to do the same for my son."

—Stephen McArdle,
former student of Lindsey Cormack